EASY to DRAW 3

ANIME & MANGA

CHIBI

This Book Belongs to:

_____

SUNLIFE DRAWING

This book will **HELP** you **EASY** to **DRAW** 20 **CUTE** Kawaii **ANIME** and **MANGA** Chibi **ANIMALS & PETS, BOYS & GIRLS**. In Japanese the word "chibi" means "small person", they have big heads, childlike creatures and very small proportions. Word "kawaii" means "pretty, lovely, charming". Chibi characters look like cute kids or baby animals and behave like adults. Even if this is your first attempt at sketching, you will not face any difficultly in **DRAWING**, using easy to follow **STEP-BY-STEP** illustrations.

Also you will find **ALL** the **CHARACTERS** for **FUN COLORING**. They are printed on one side of a page for easy removal and displaying of your own artistic work.

Enjoy DRAWING & COLORING!

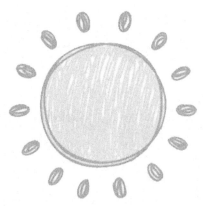

E-mail: SunlifeDrawing@gmail.com
Twitter: @SunlifeDrawing
Amazon Author's Page: Amazon.com/author/sunlifedrawing

CONTENTS:

CHIBI RABBIT

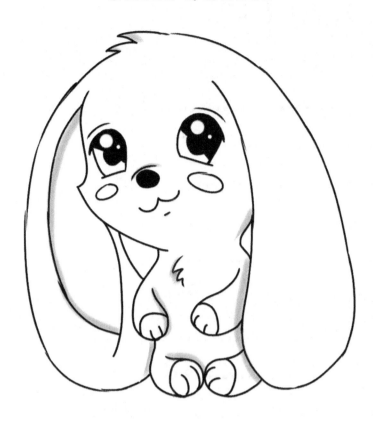

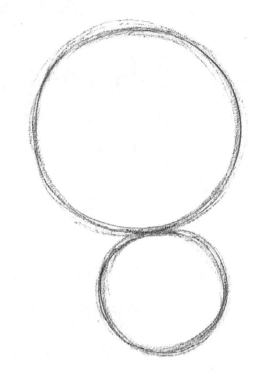

2.

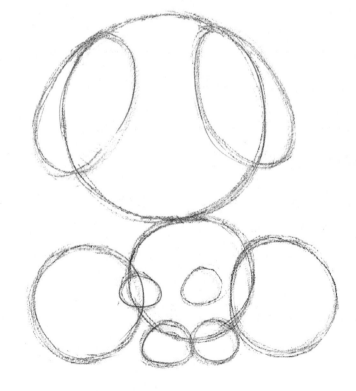

3.

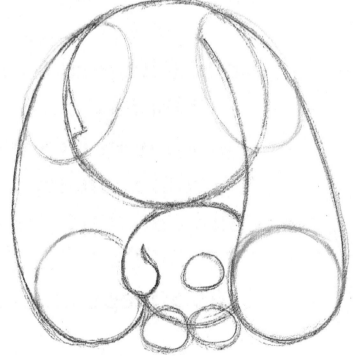

4.

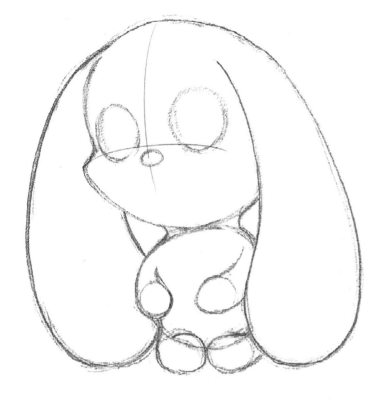

5.

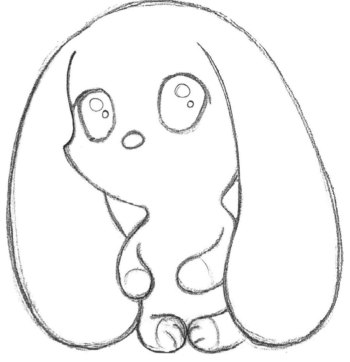

6.

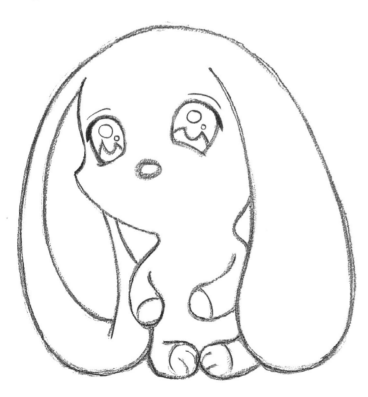

7.

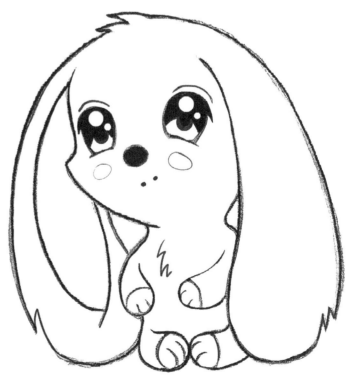

CHIBI JOYFUL GIRL

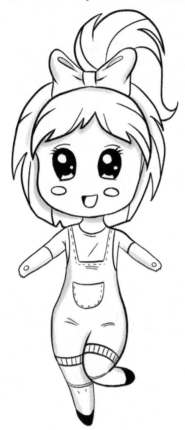

1.

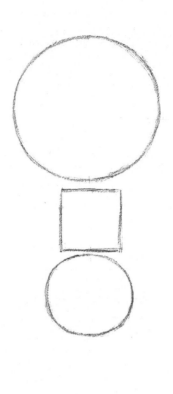

2.

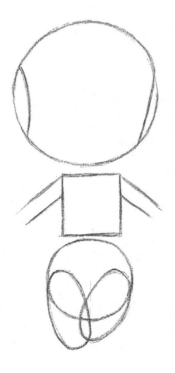

3.

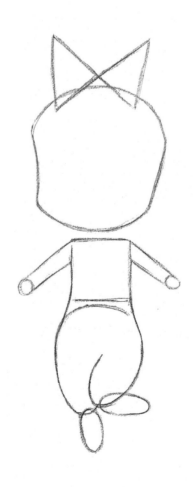

4.

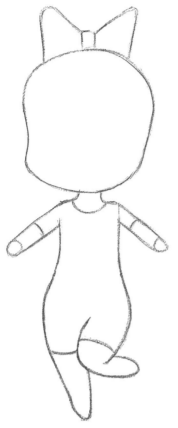

5.

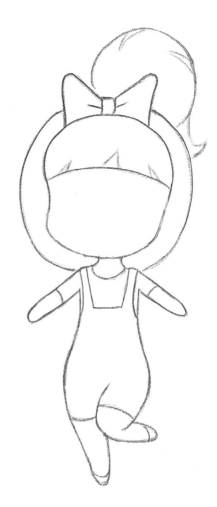

6.

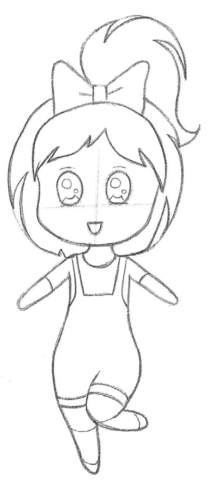

7.

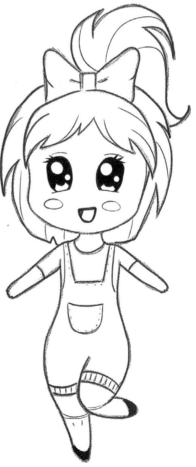

CHIBI UNICORN

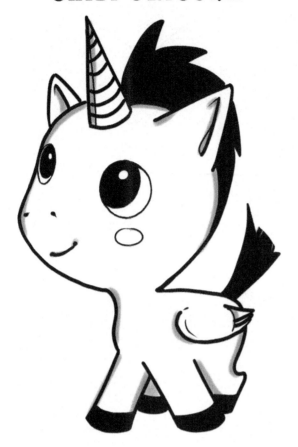

1.

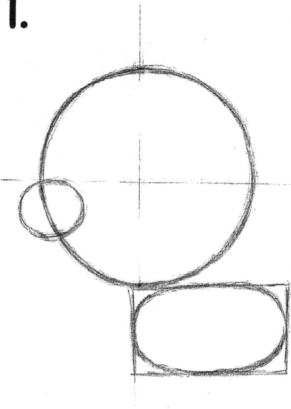

2.

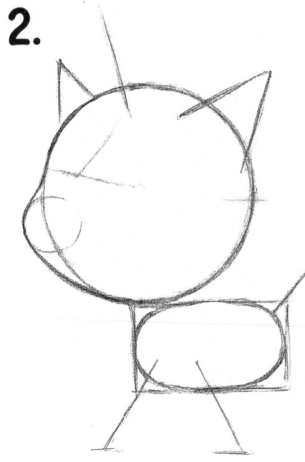

3.

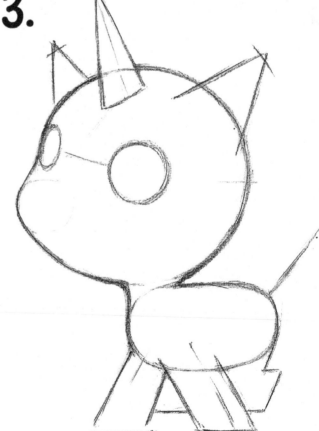

4.

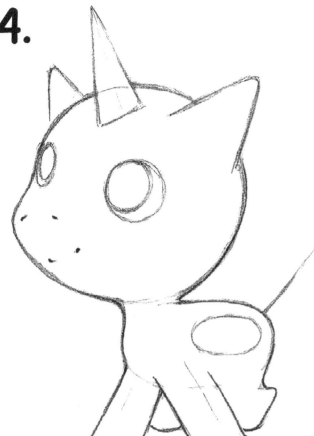

5.

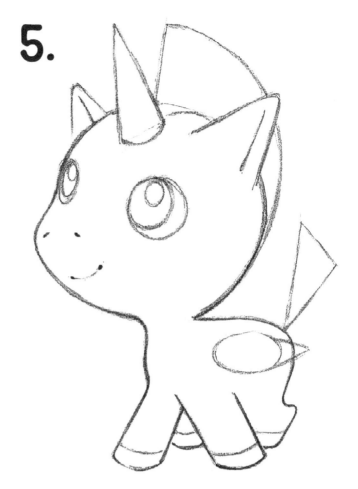

6.

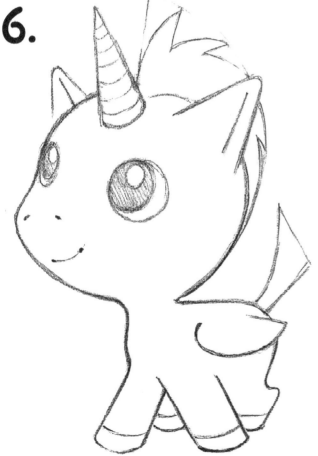

7.

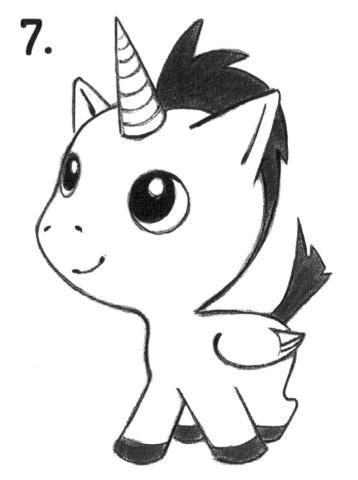

CHIBI HAPPY BOY

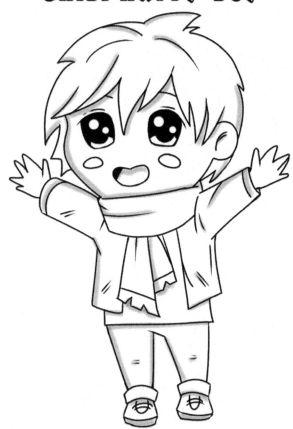

1.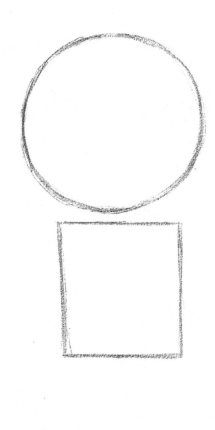

2.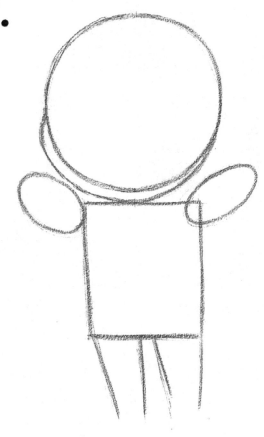

3.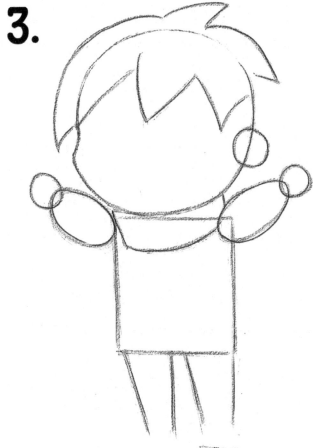

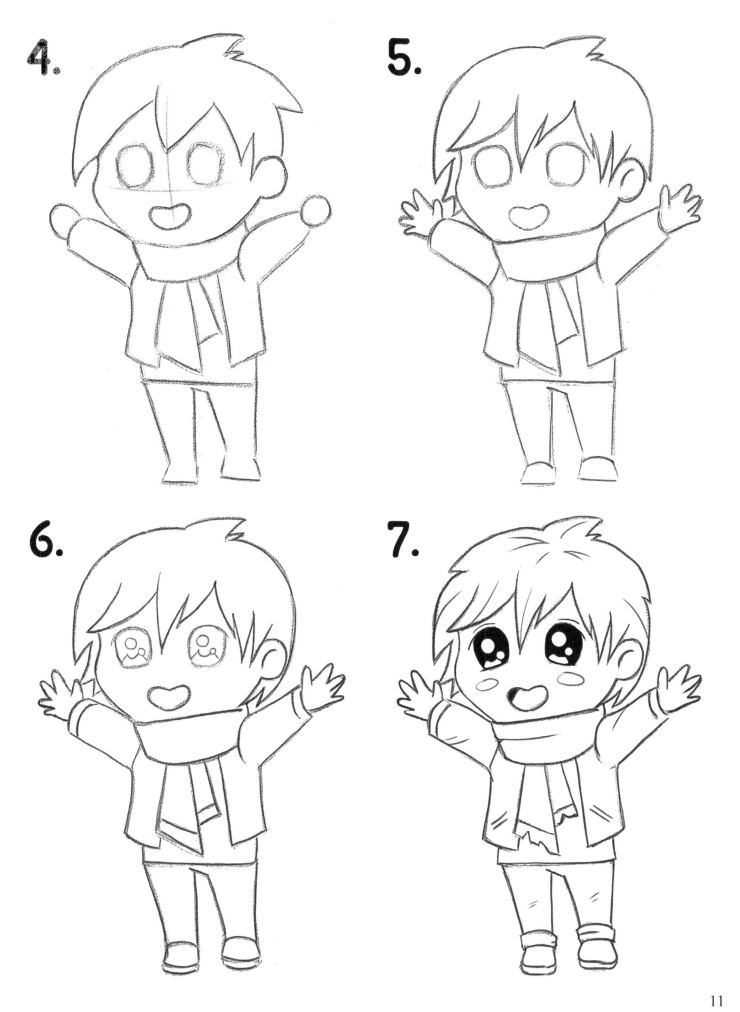

CHIBI OCTOPUS

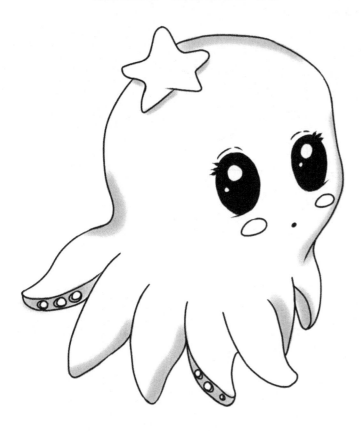

1.

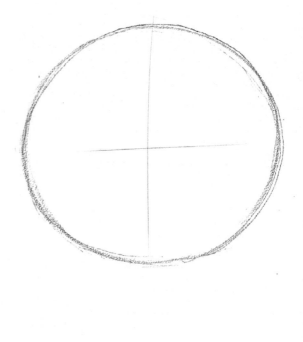

2.

3.

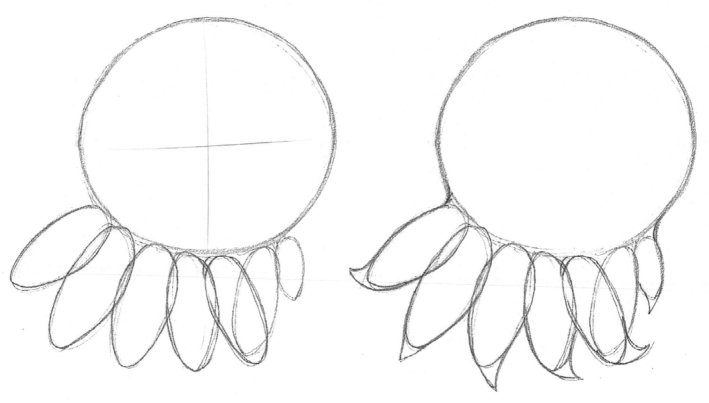

4.

5.

6.

7.

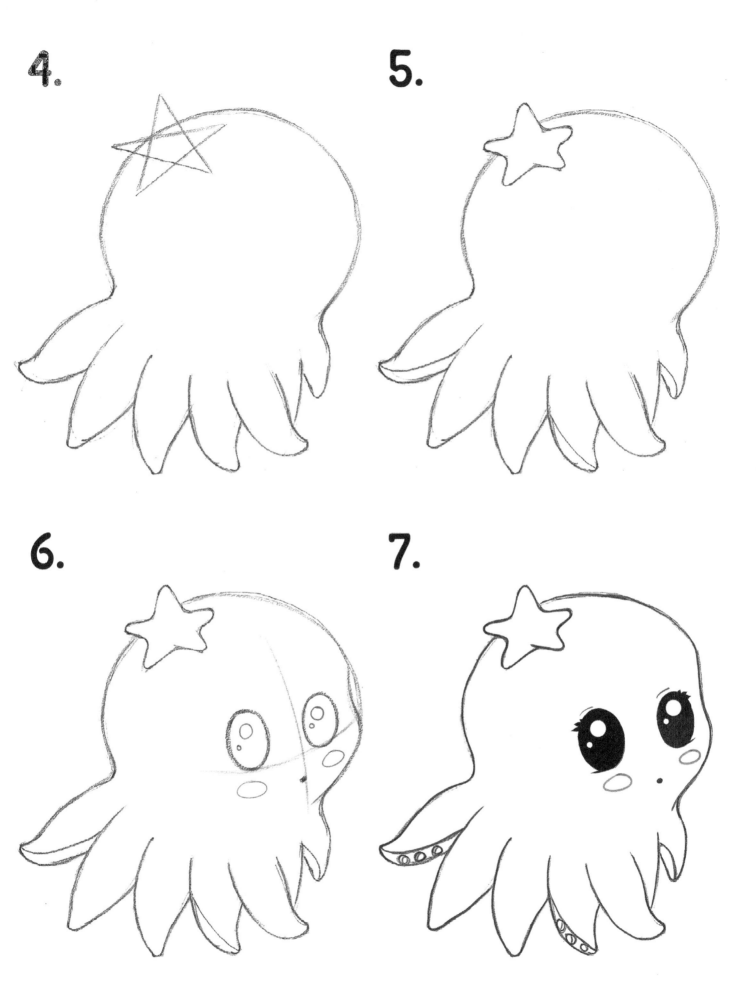

CHIBI FOX GIRL

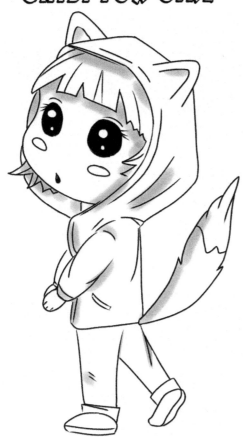

1.

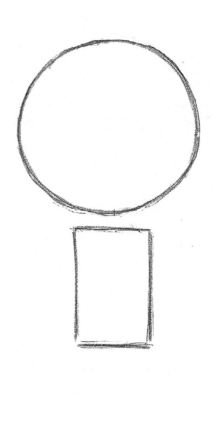

2.

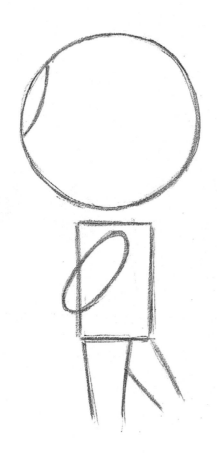

3.

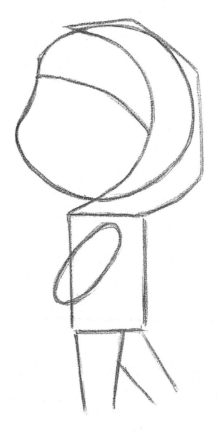

4.

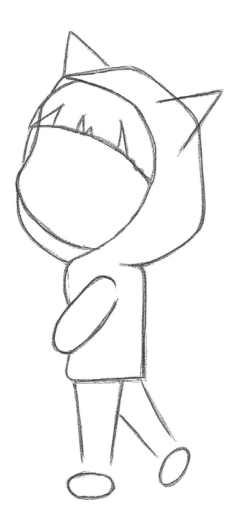

5.

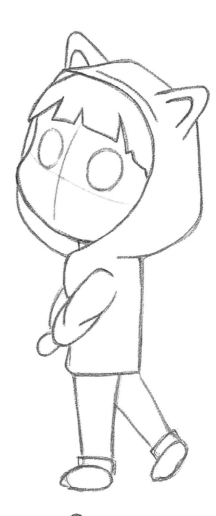

6.

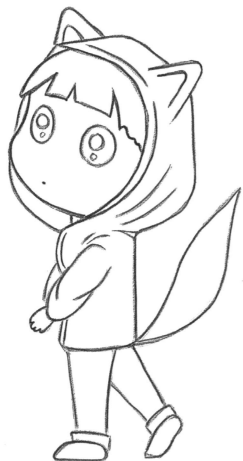

7.

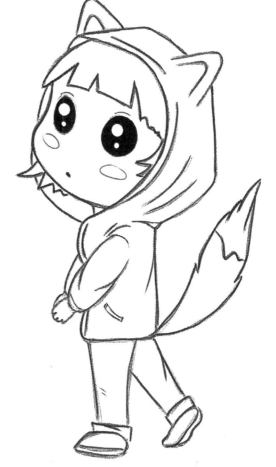

CHIBI RACCOON

1.

2.

3.

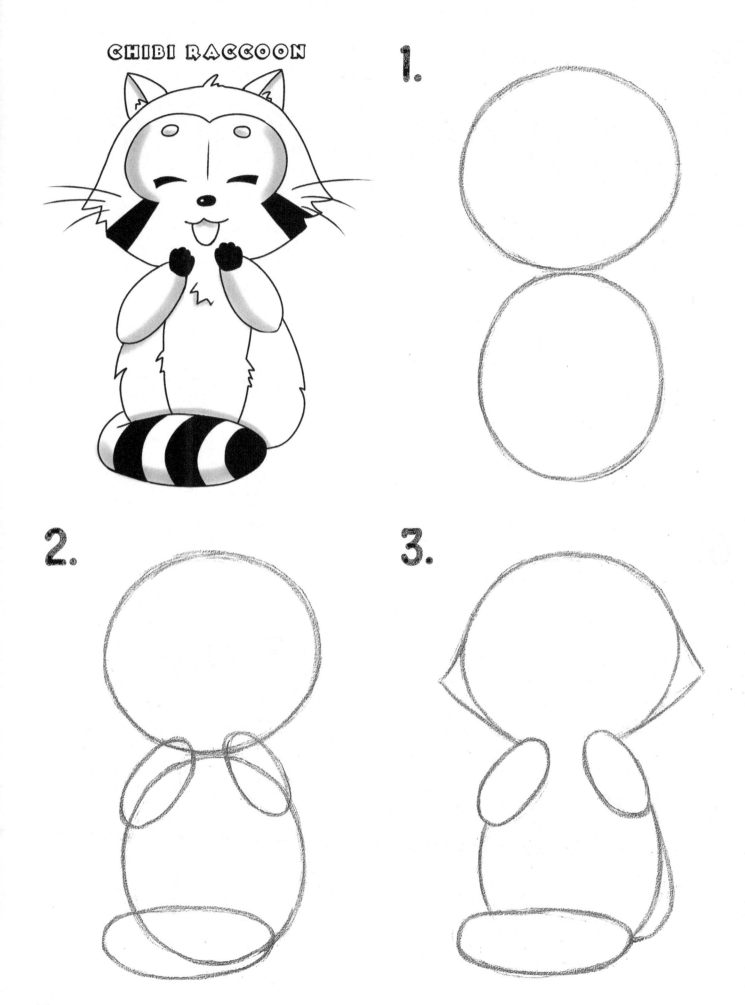

4.

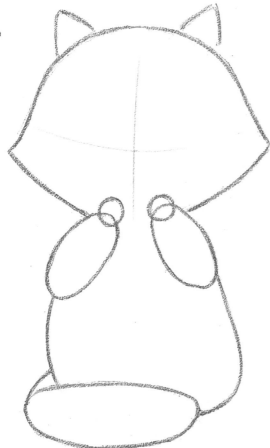

5.

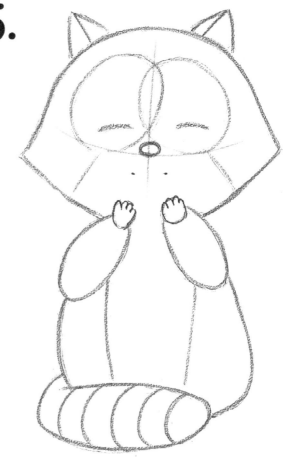

6.

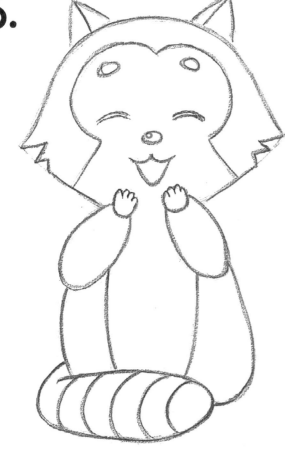

7.

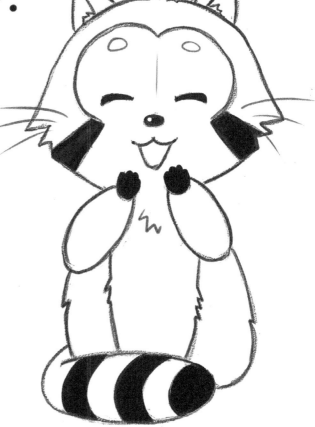

CHIBI BAD BOY

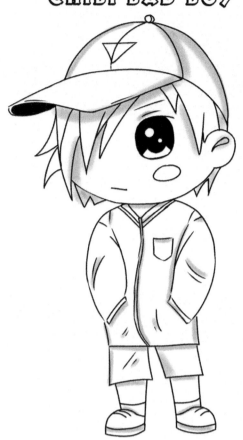

1.

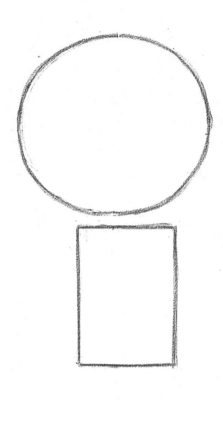

2.

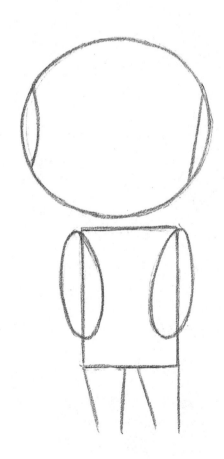

3.

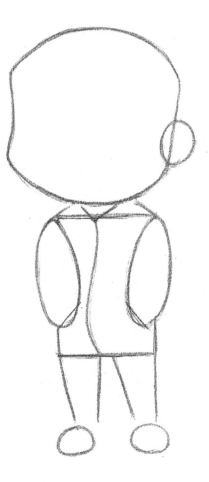

4.

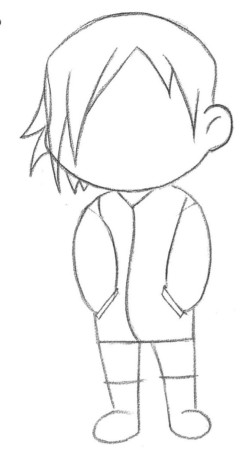

5.

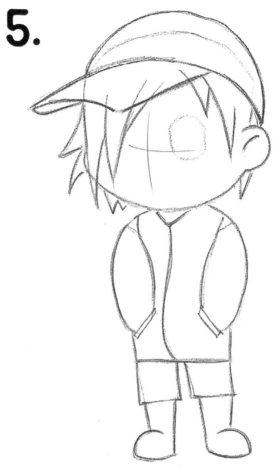

6.

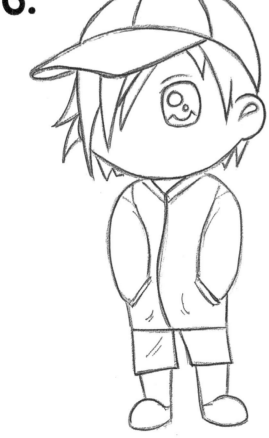

7.

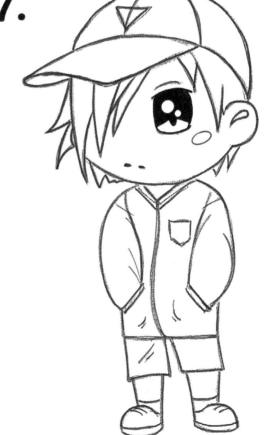

CHIBI DOG

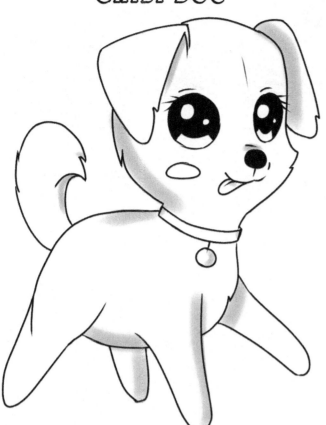

1.

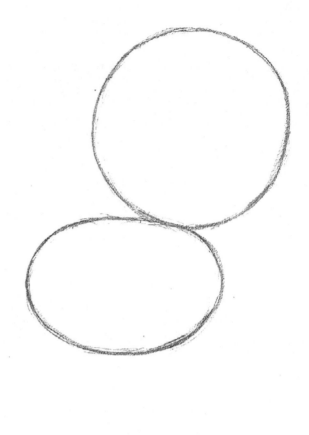

2.

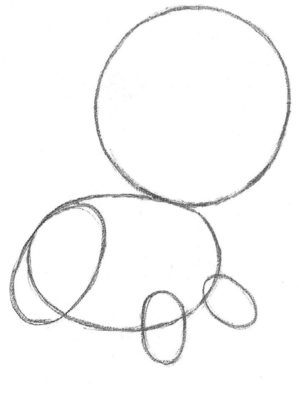

3.

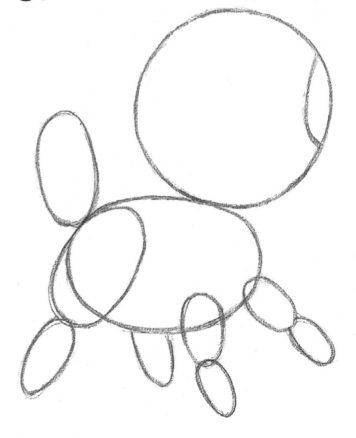

4.

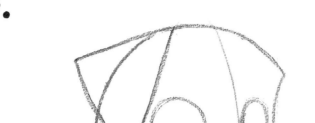
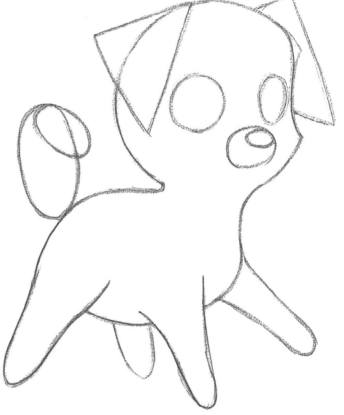

5.

6.

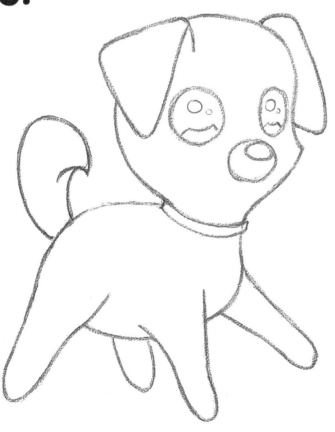

7.

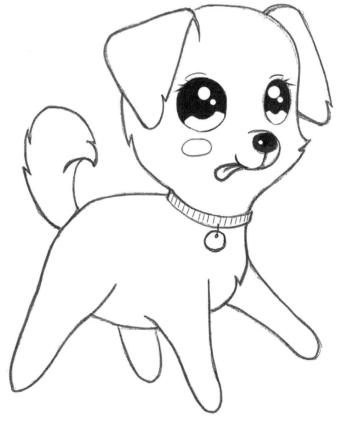

CHIBI CAT GIRL

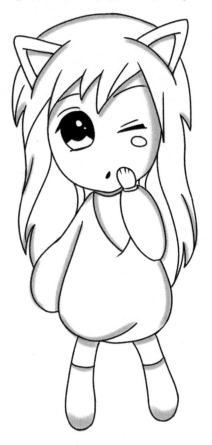

1.

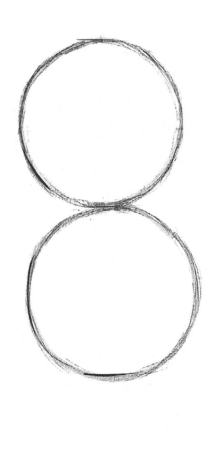

2.

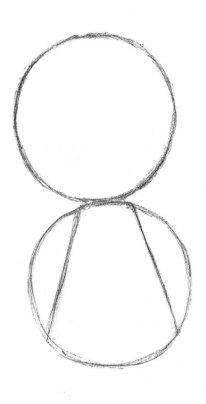

3.

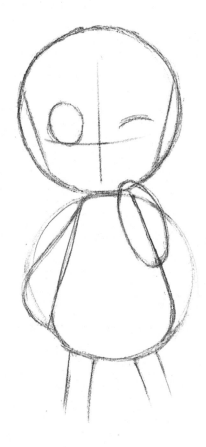

4.

5.

6.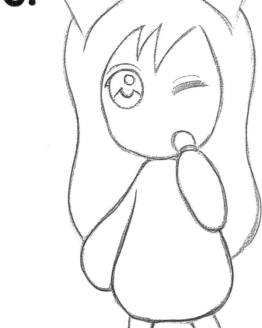

7.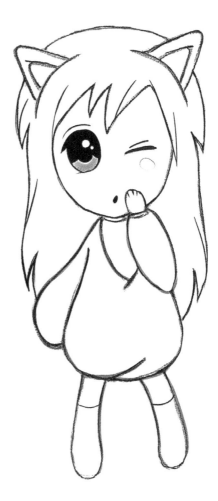

CHIBI PARROT

1.

2.

3.

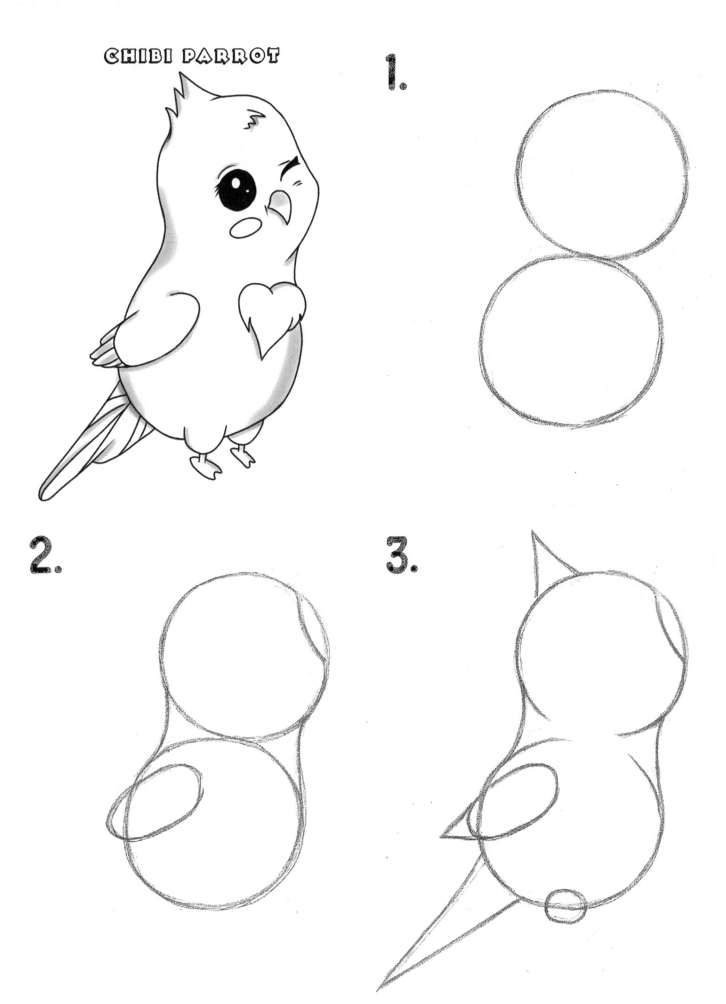

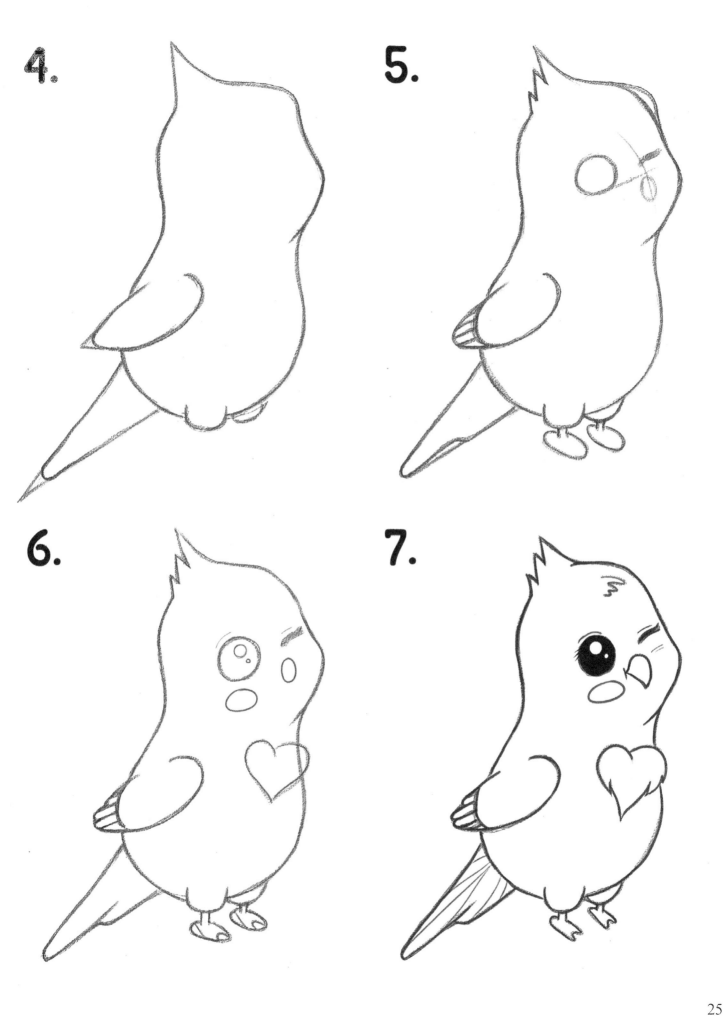

CHIBI LAUGHING BOY

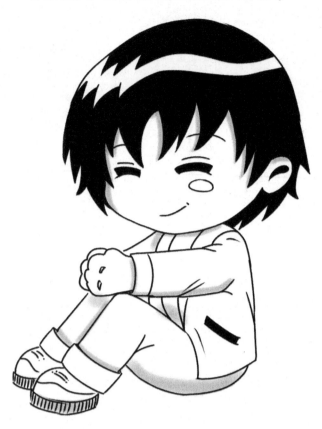

1.

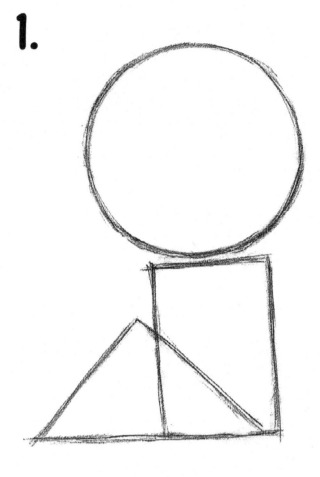

2.

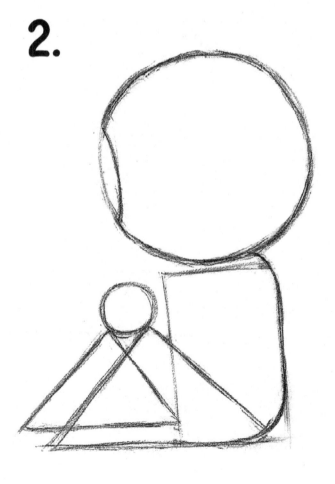

3.

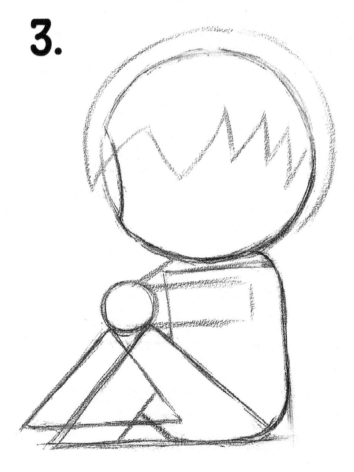

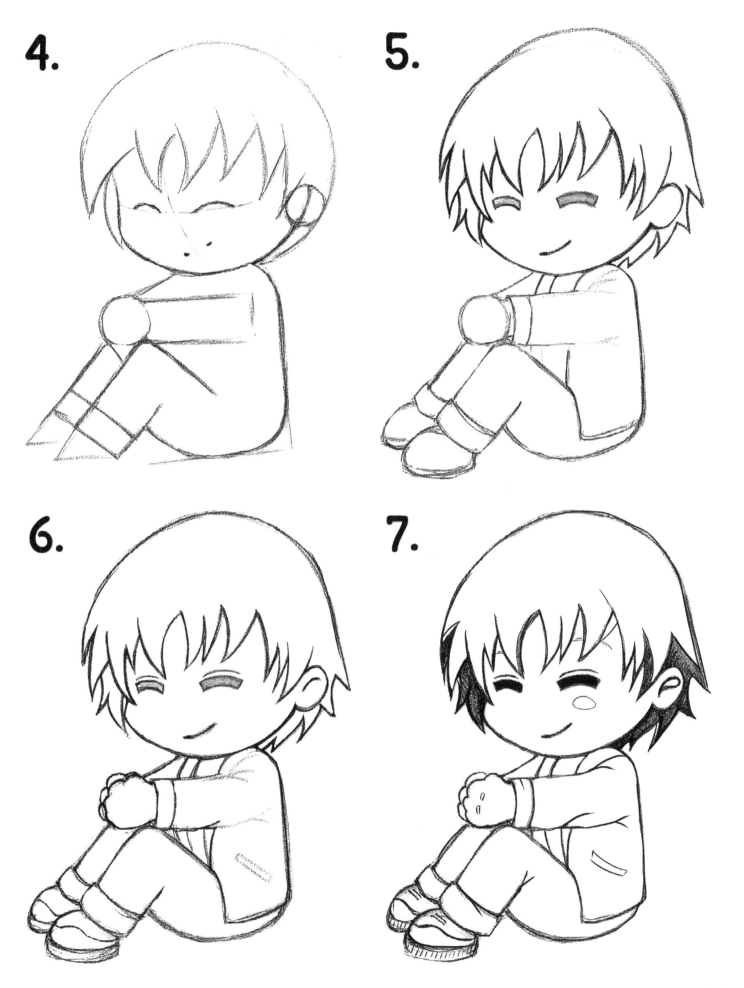

CHIBI CAT

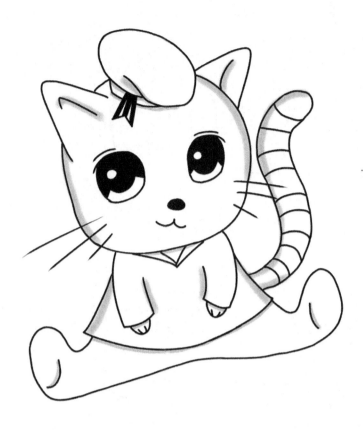

 1.

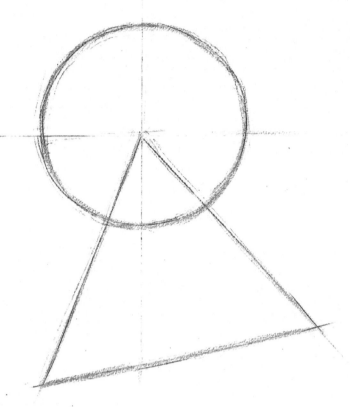

2.

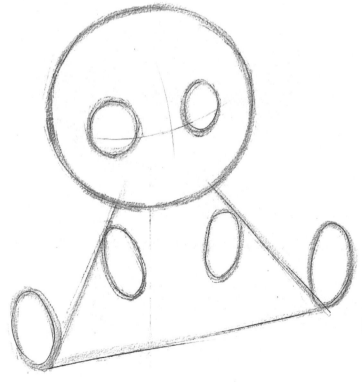

3.

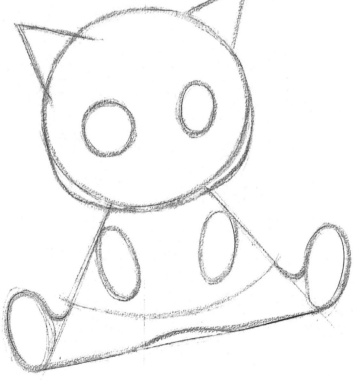

4.

5.

6.

7.

CHIBI OFFENDED GIRL

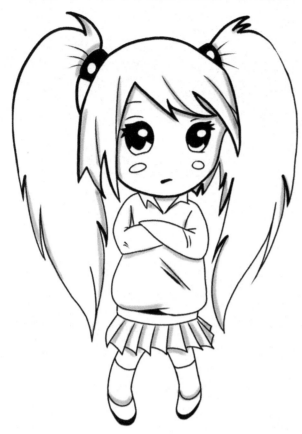

1.

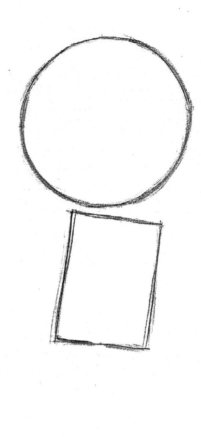

2.

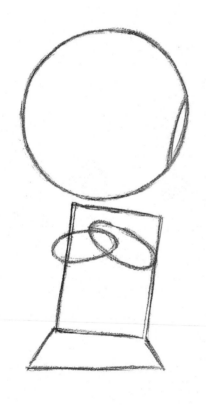

3.

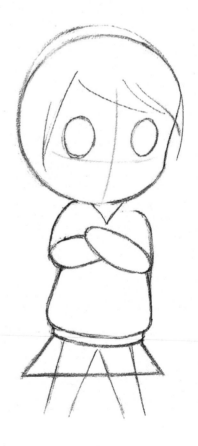

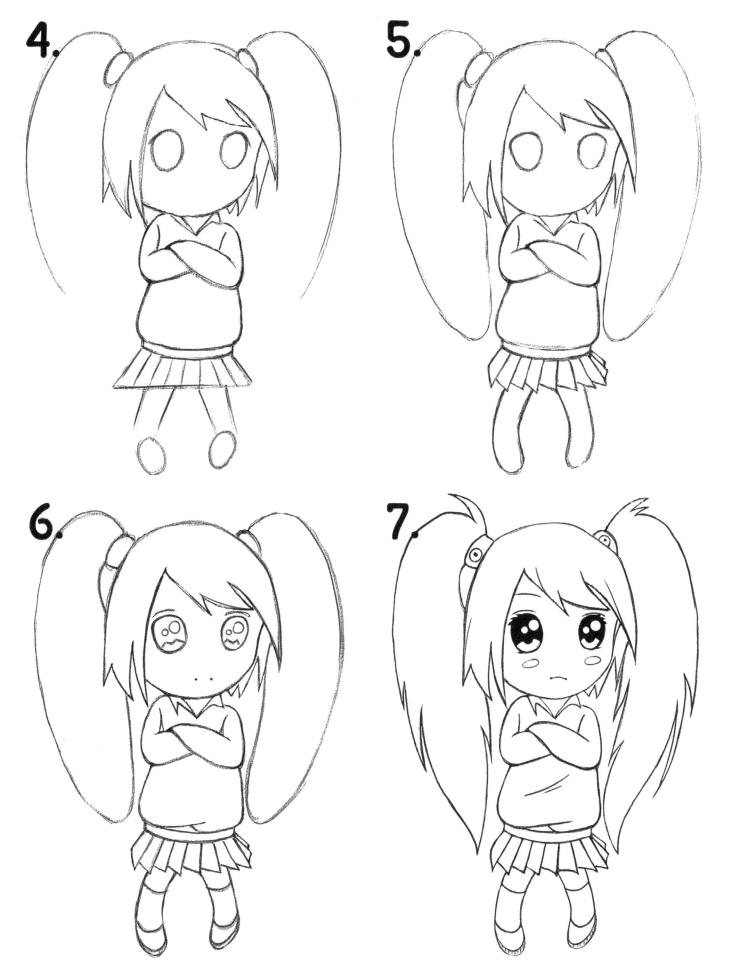

4.

5.

6.

7.

CHIBI FOX

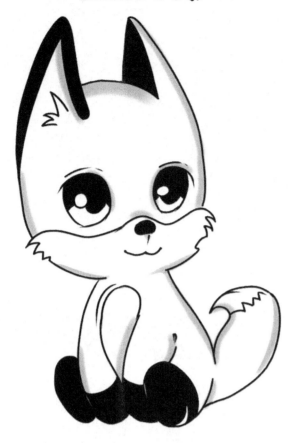

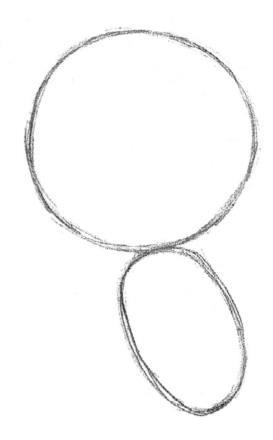

2.

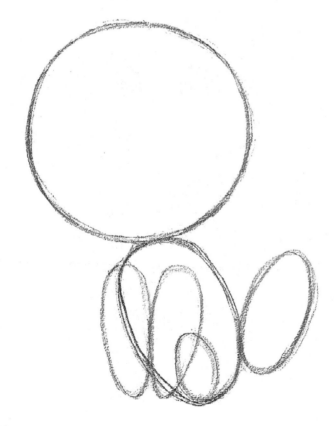

3.

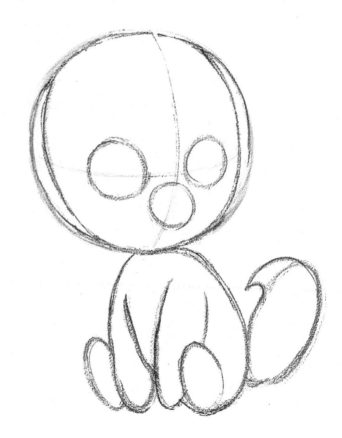

4.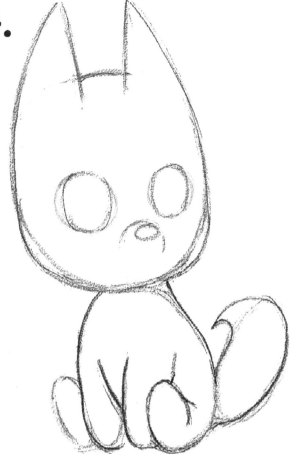

5.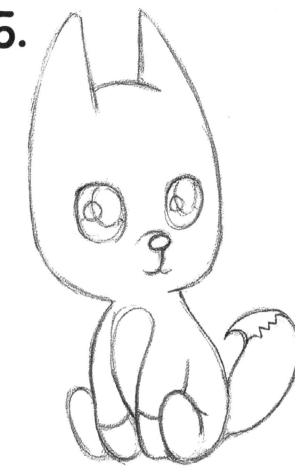

6.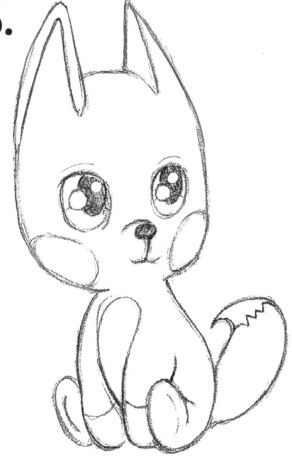

7.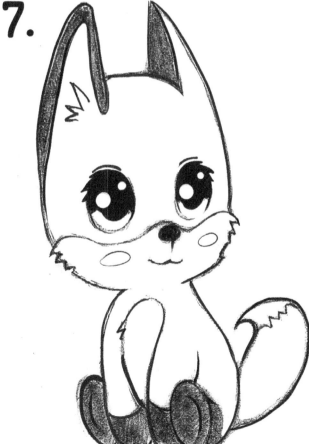

CHIBI BOY IN HEADPHONES

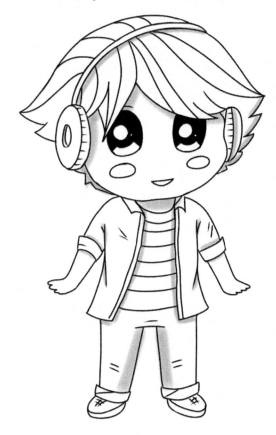

1.

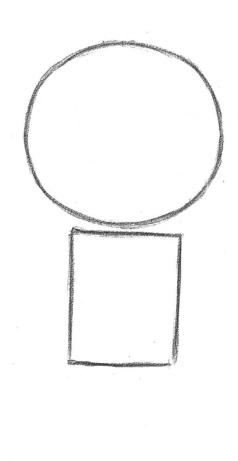

2.

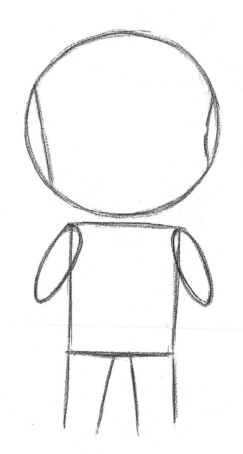

3.

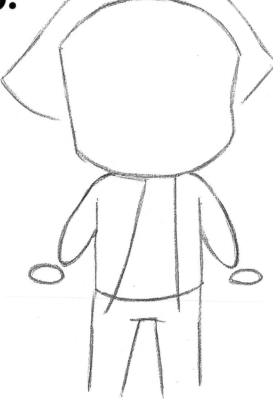

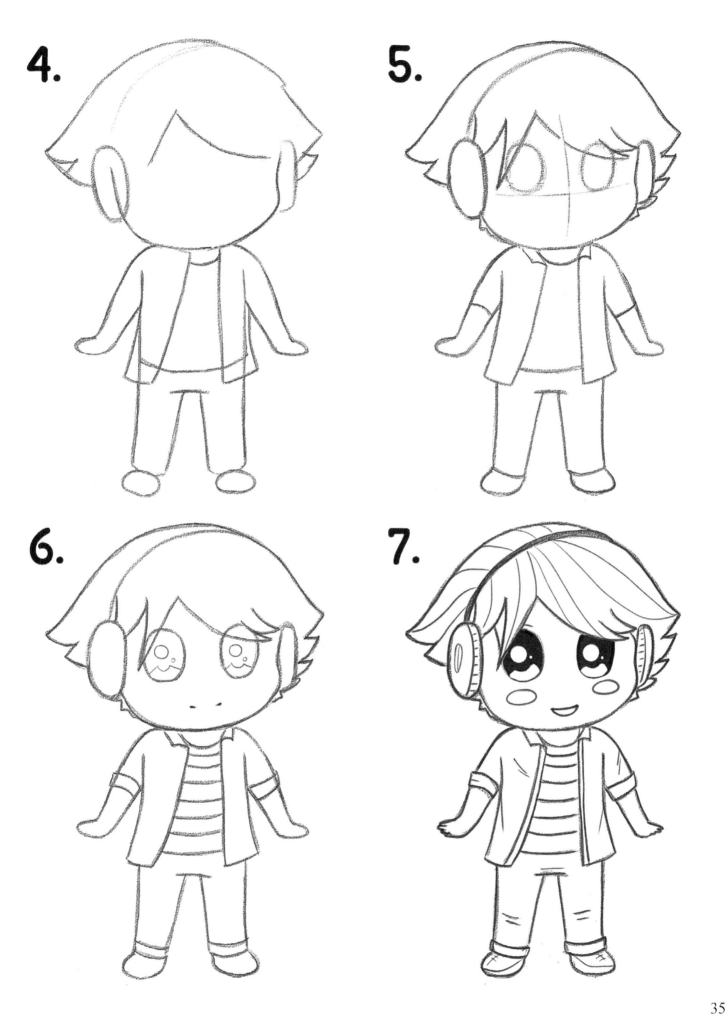

4.

5.

6.

7.

CHIBI HAMSTER

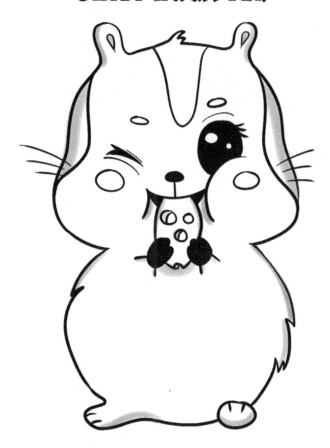

 1.

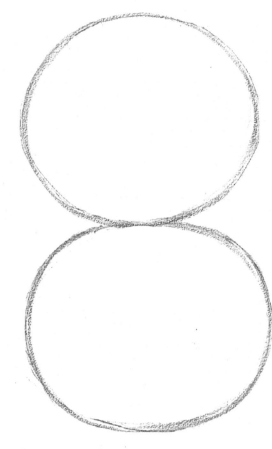

2.

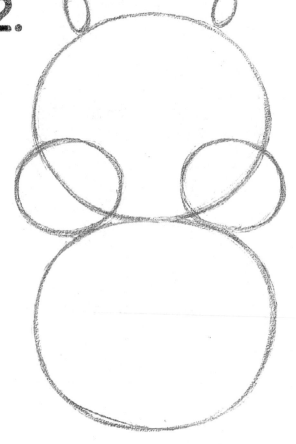

3.

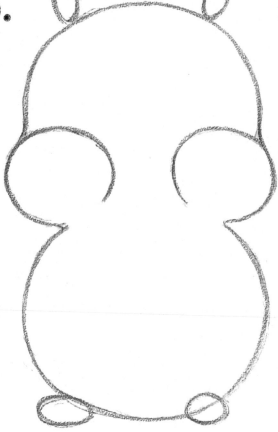

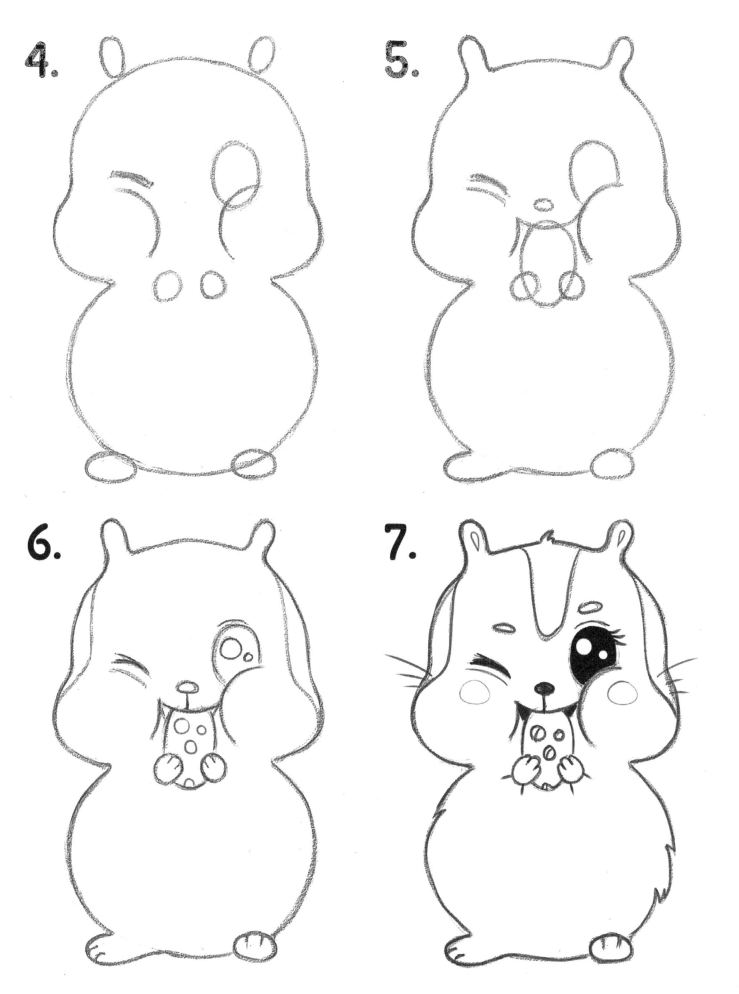

4. **5.** **6.** **7.**

CHIBI CUTE GIRL

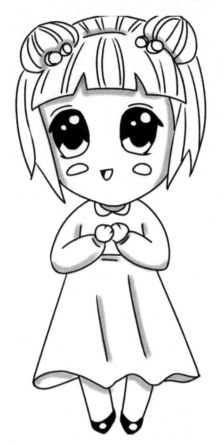

1.

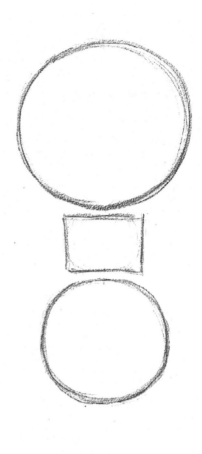

2.

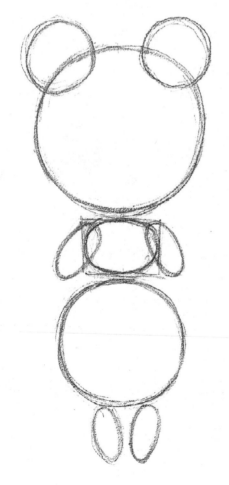

3.

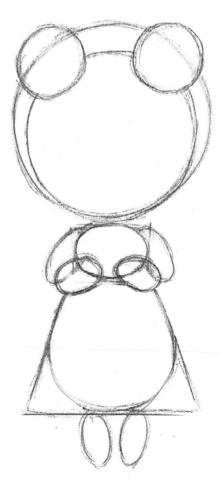

4.

5.

6.

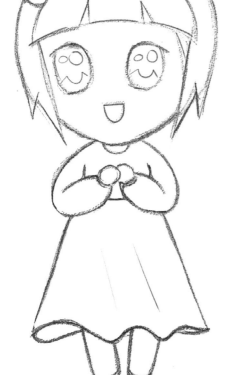

7.

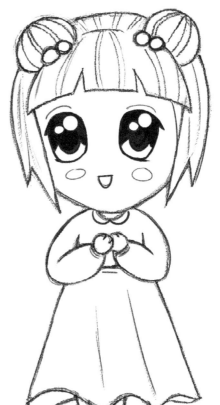

CHIBI OWL

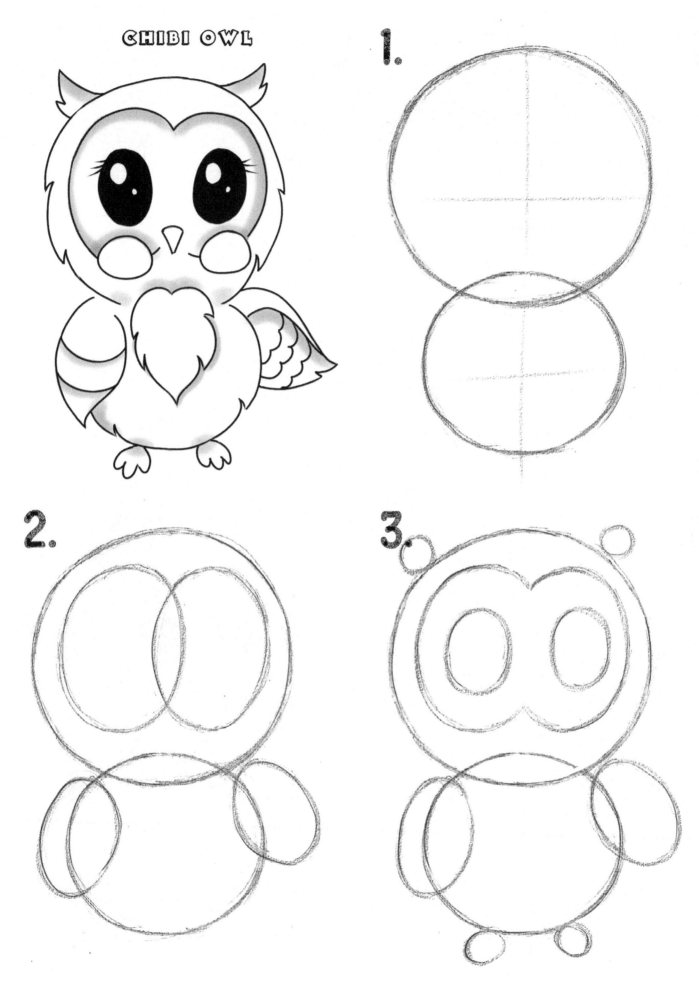

1.

2.

3.

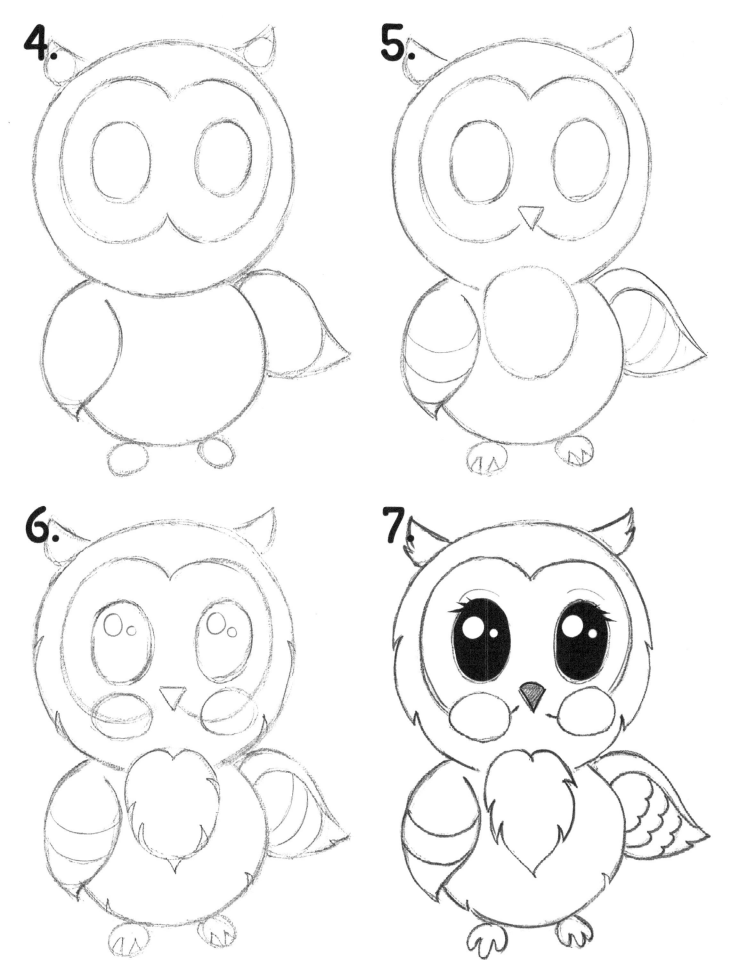

CHIBI SHEEP

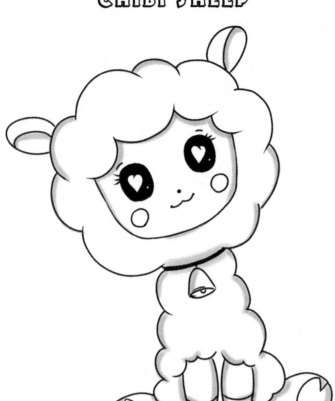

1.

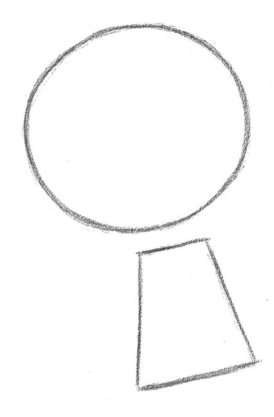

2.

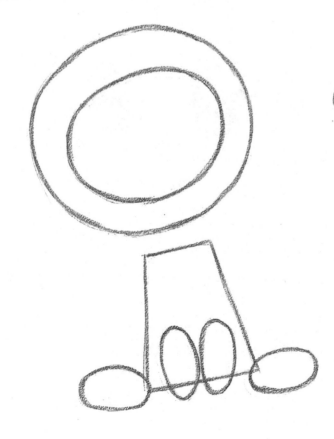

3.

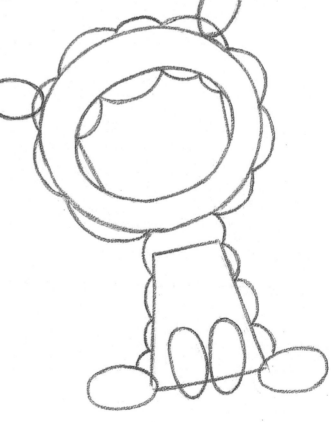

4.

5.

6.

7.

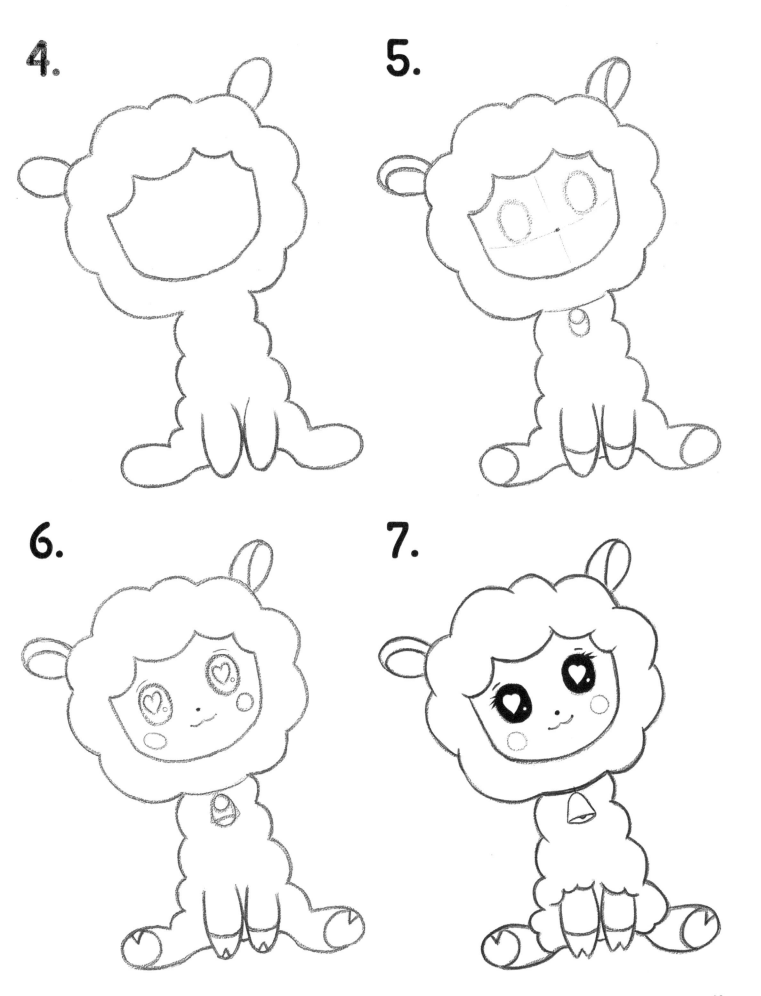

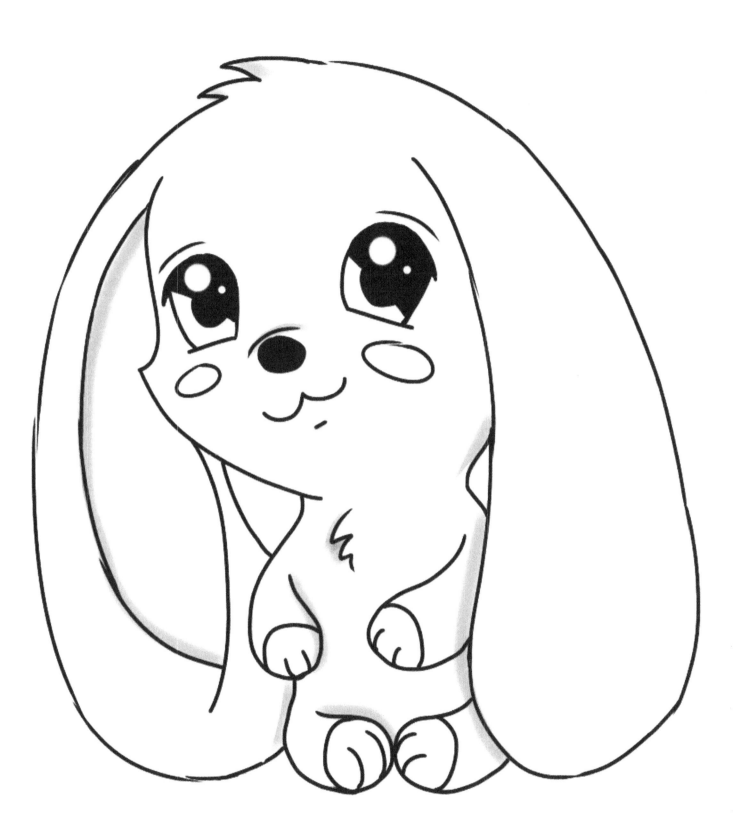

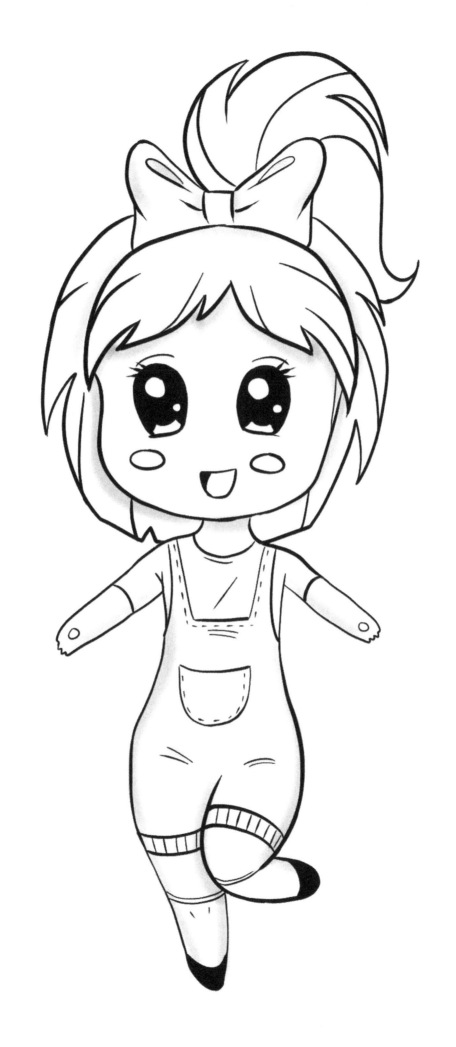

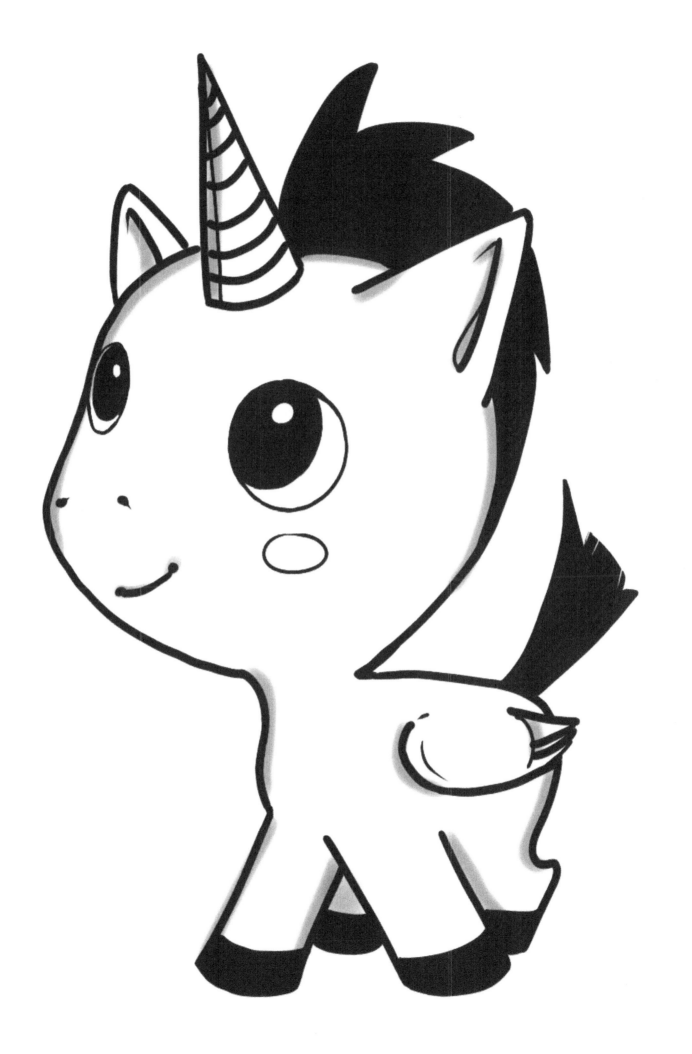

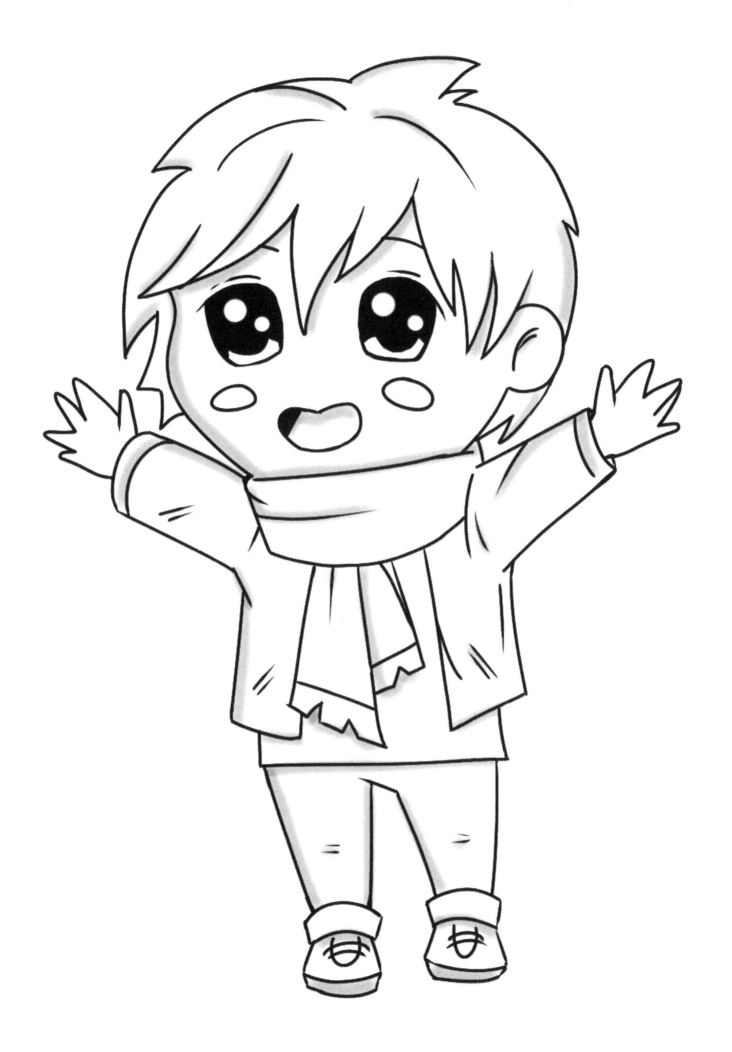

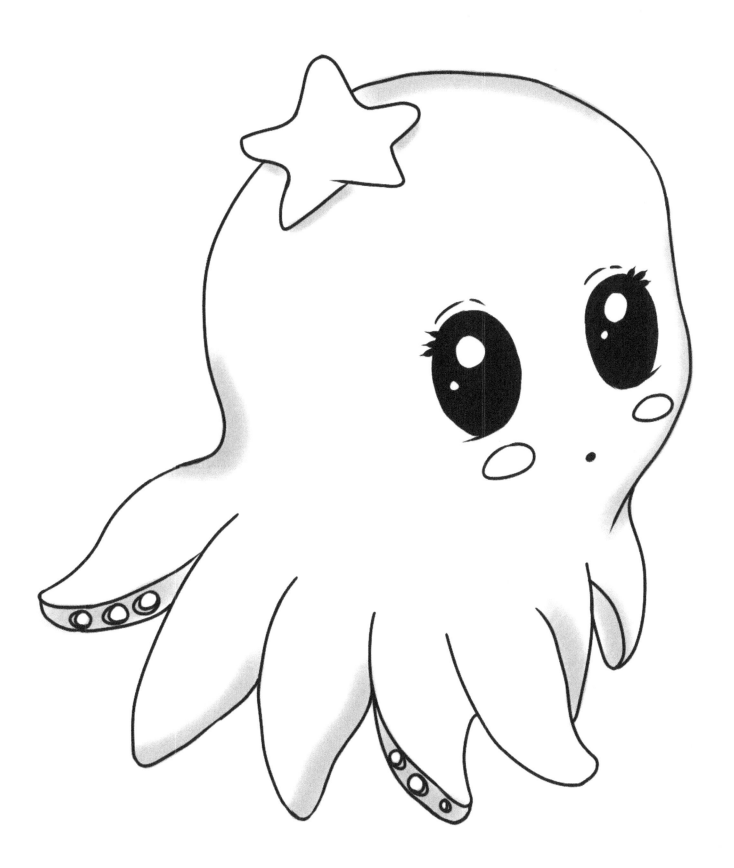

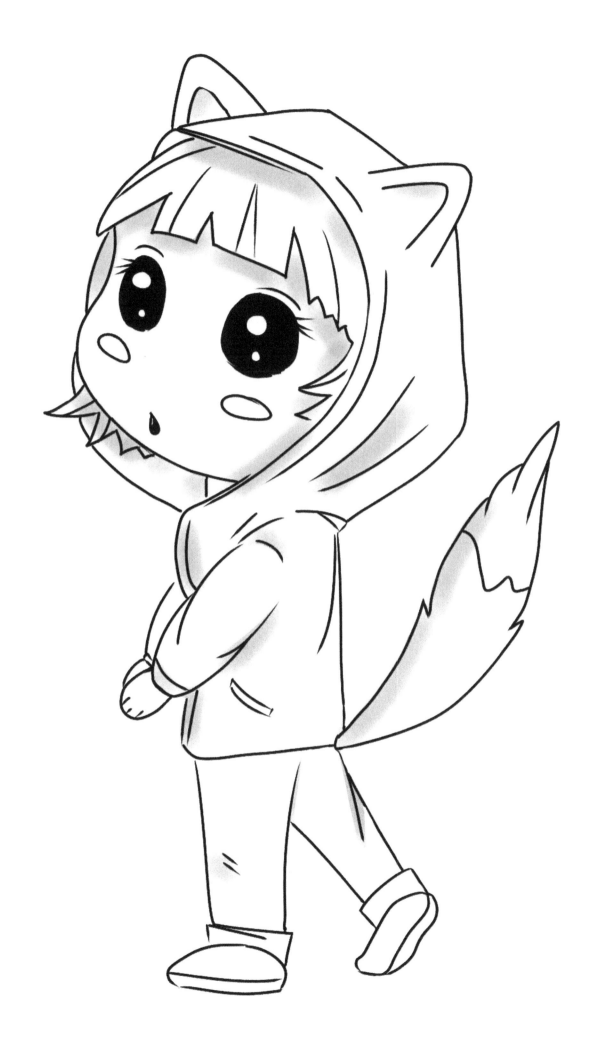

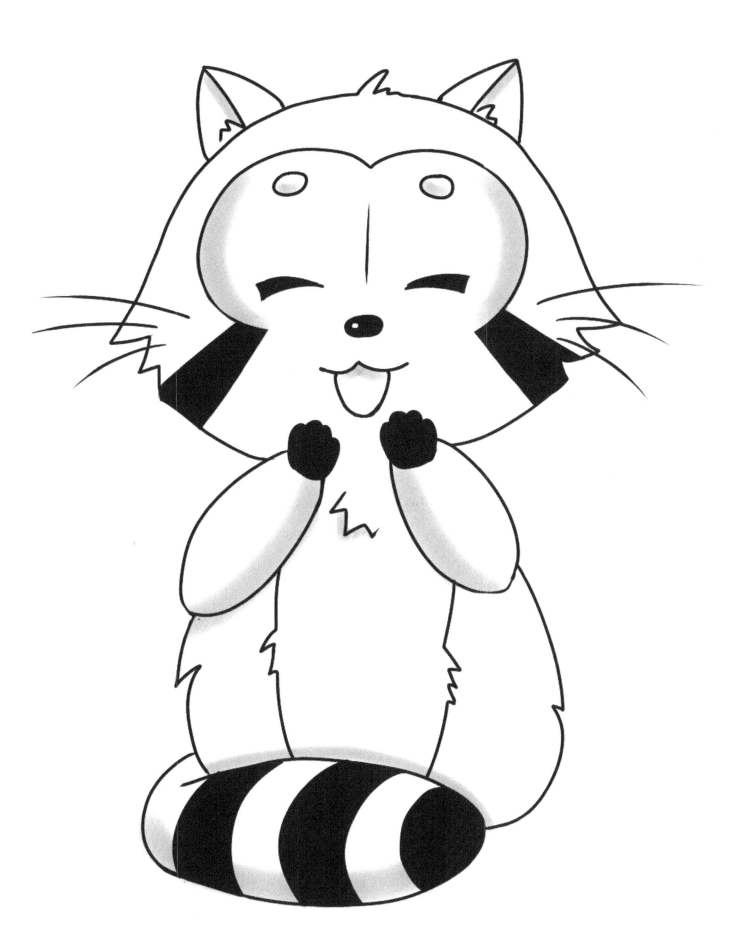

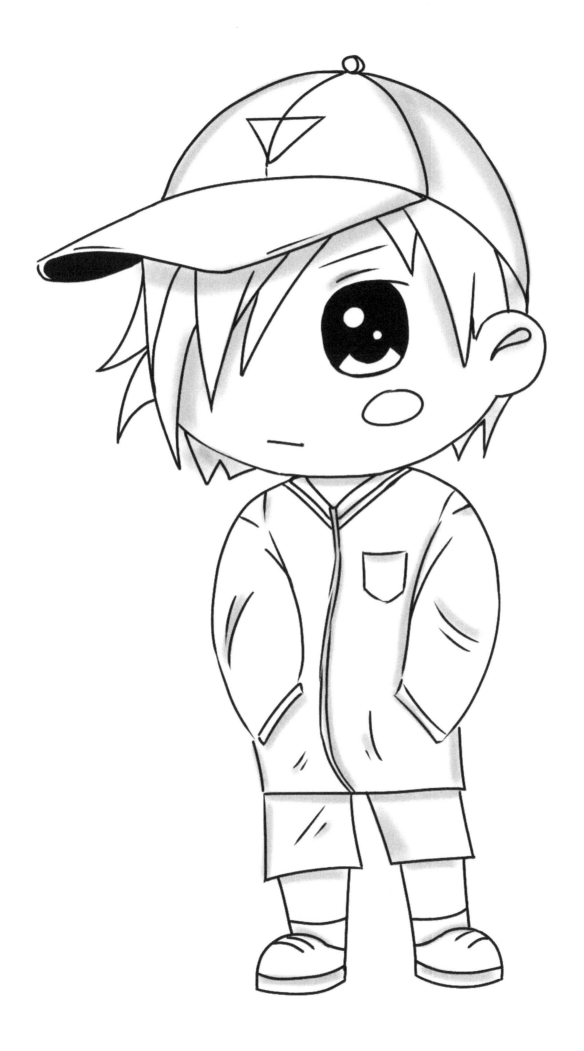

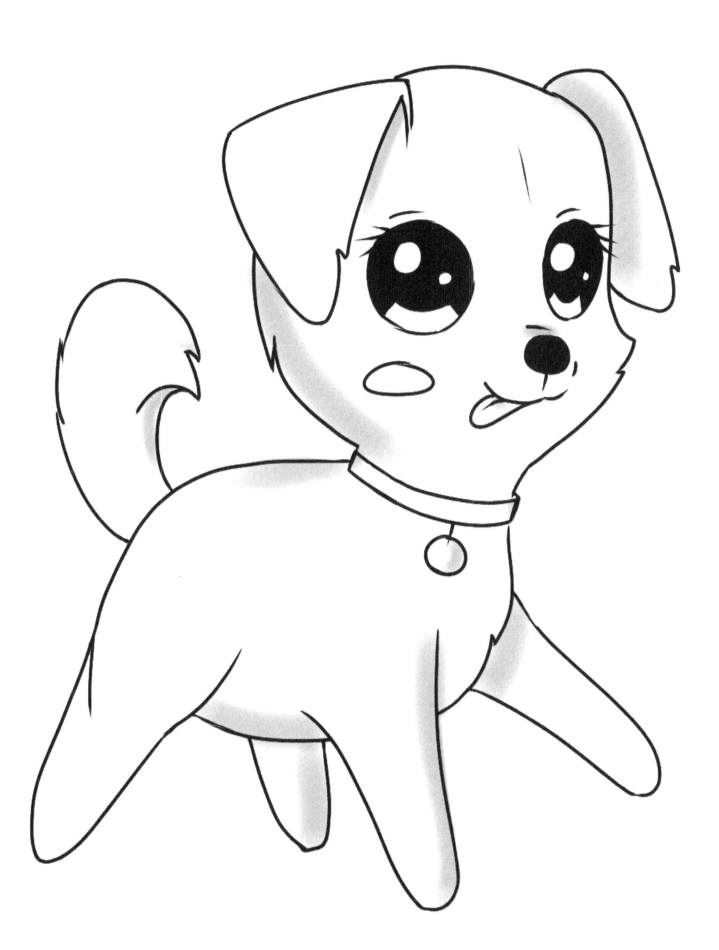

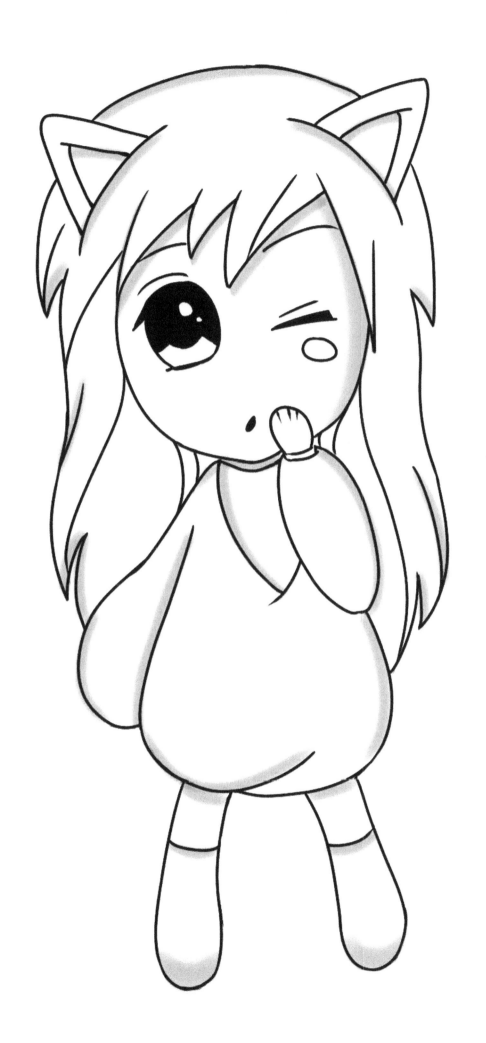

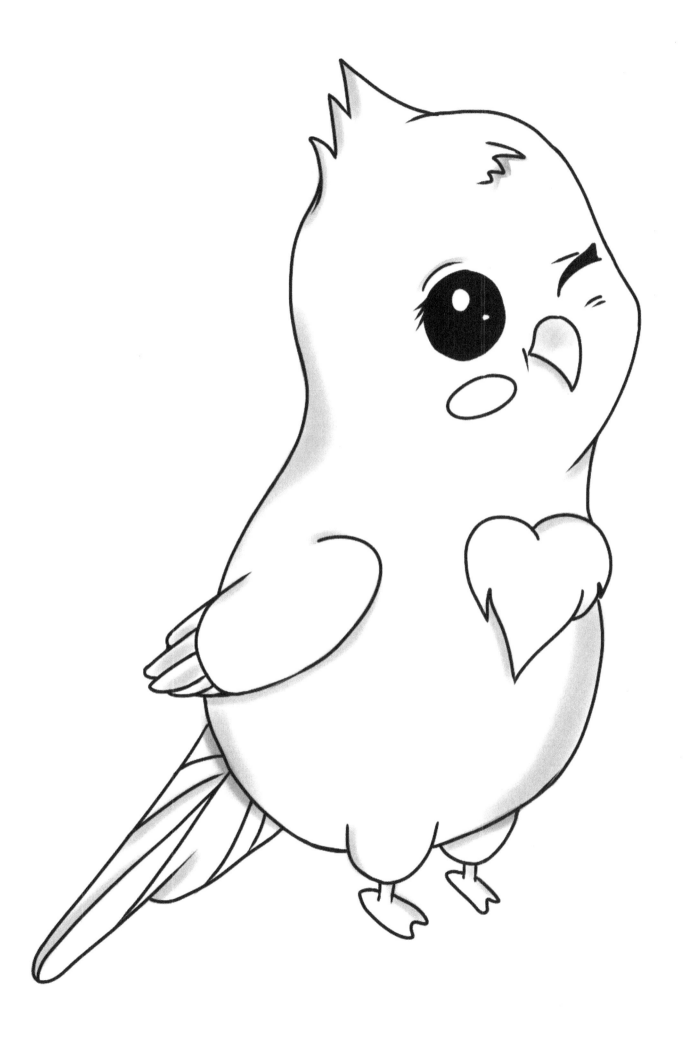

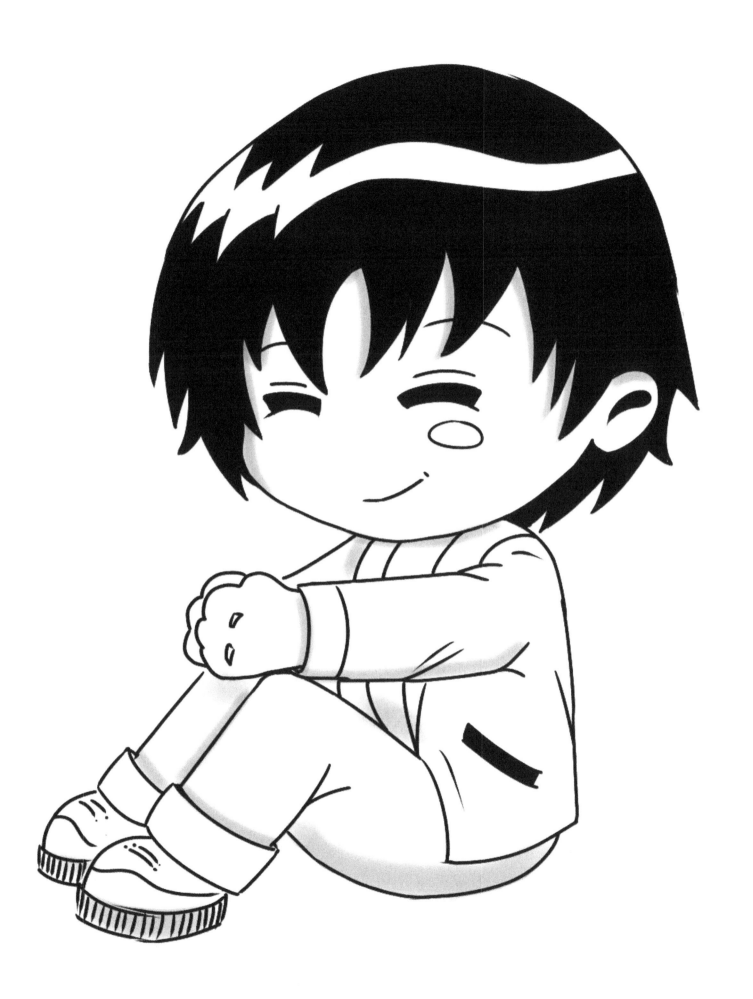

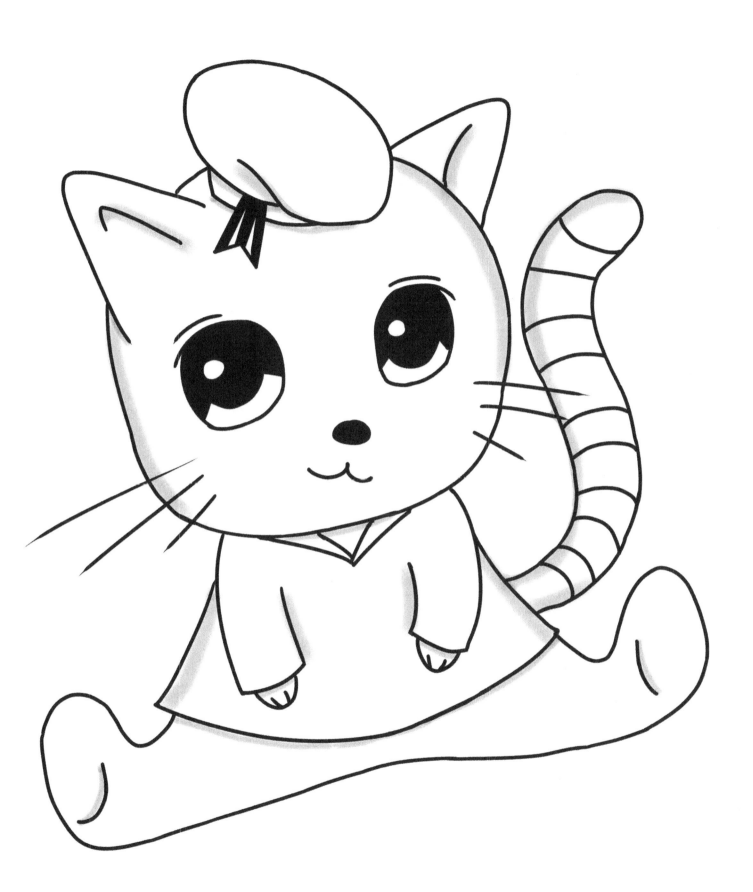

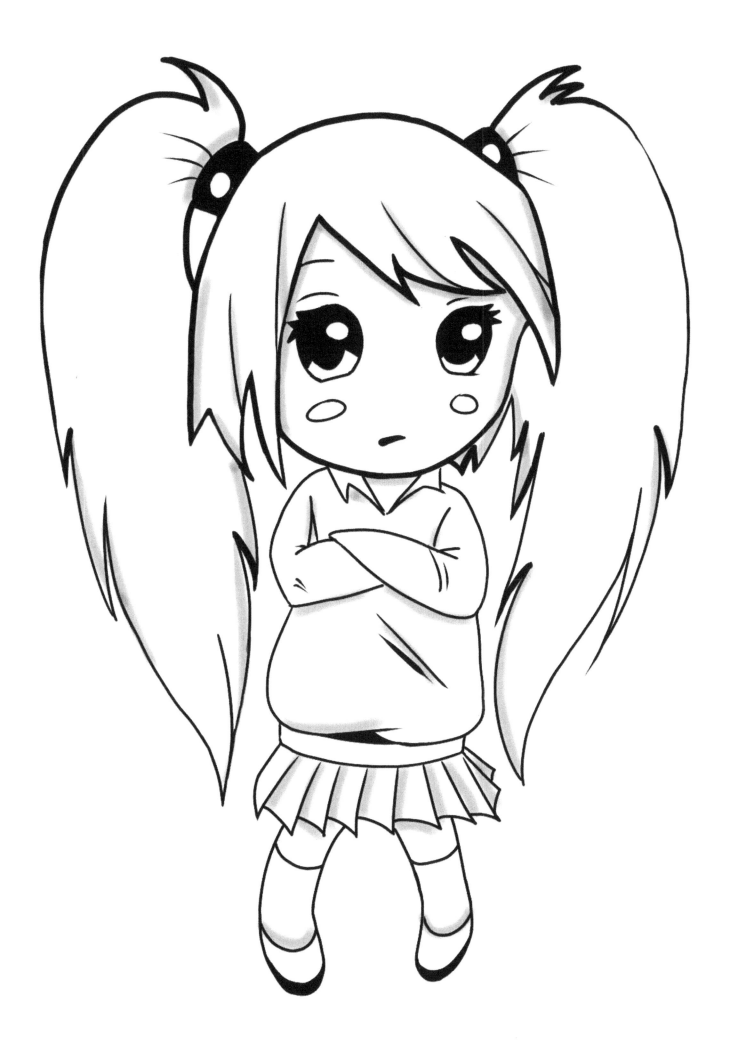

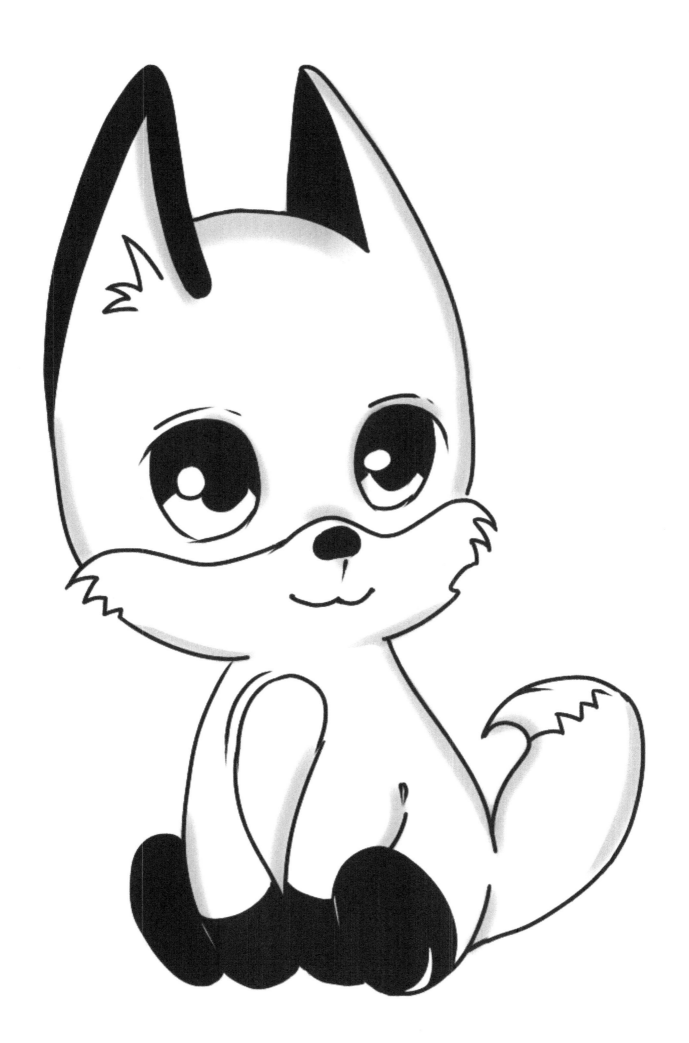

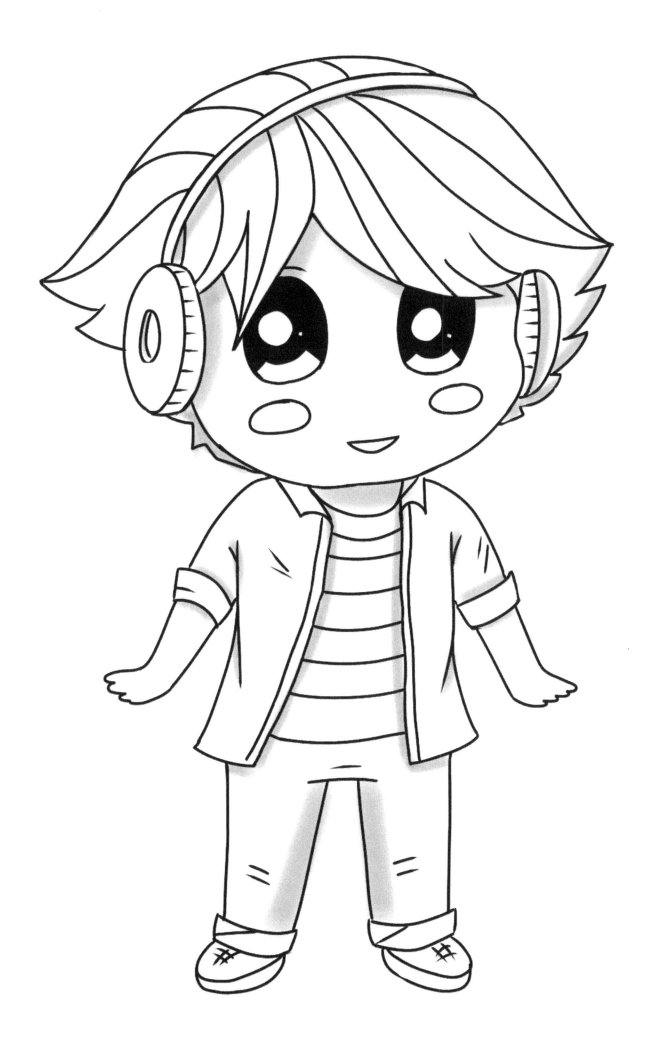

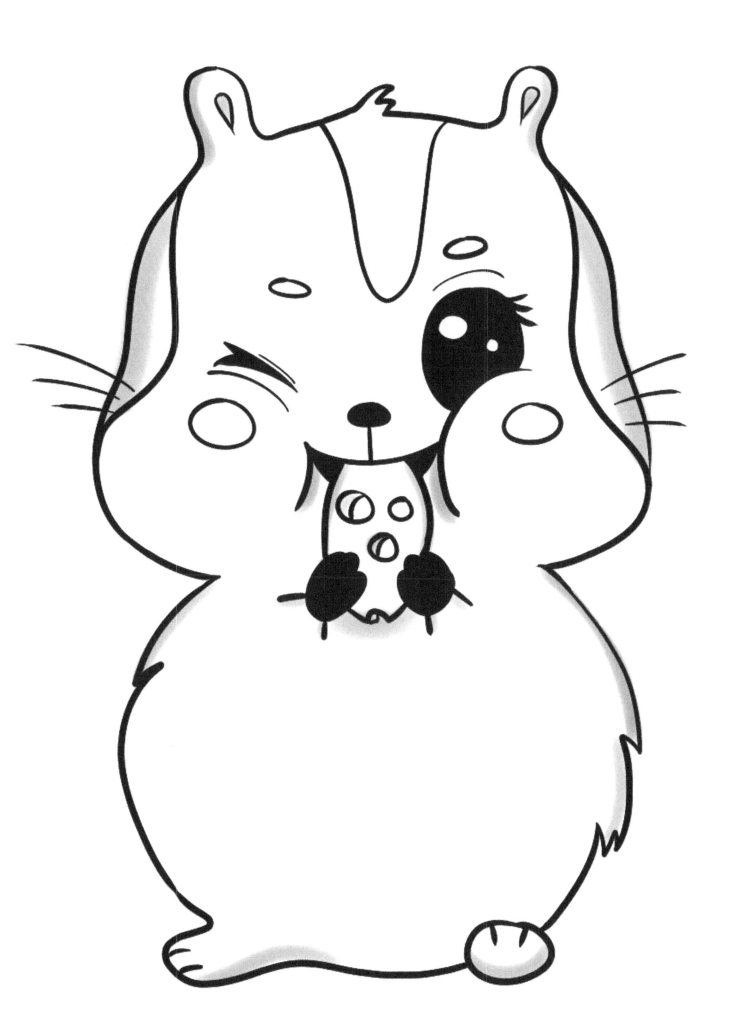

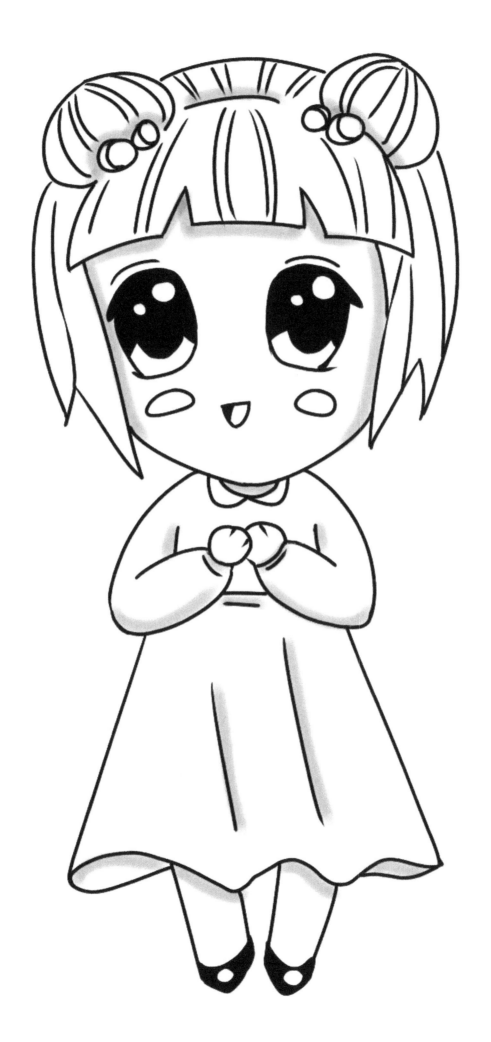

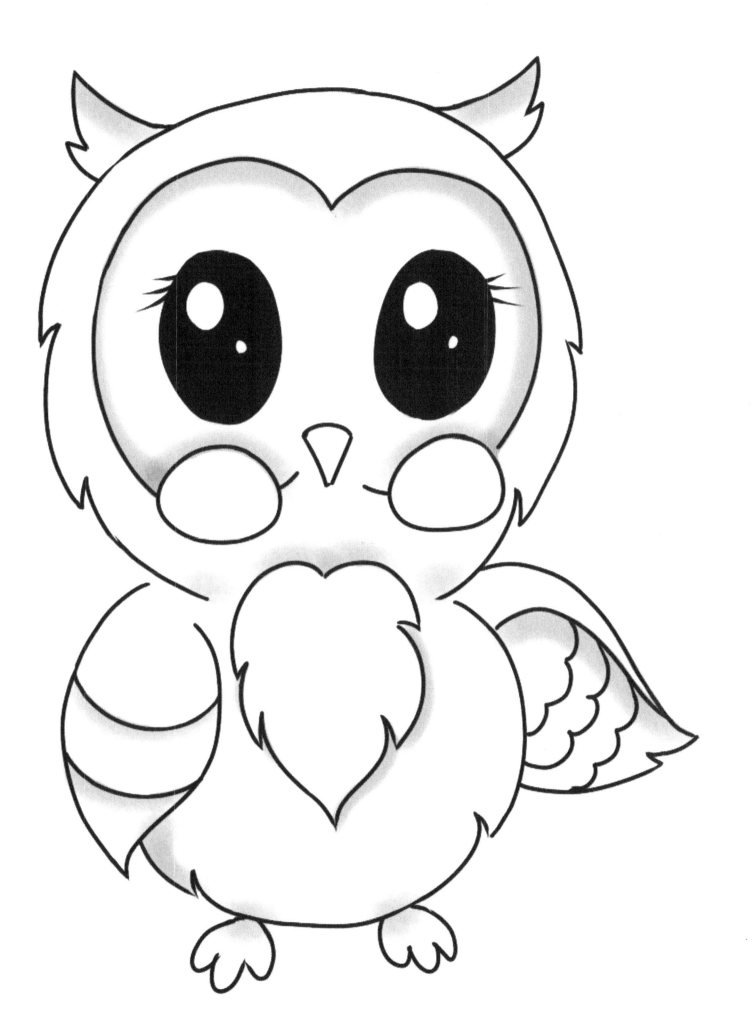

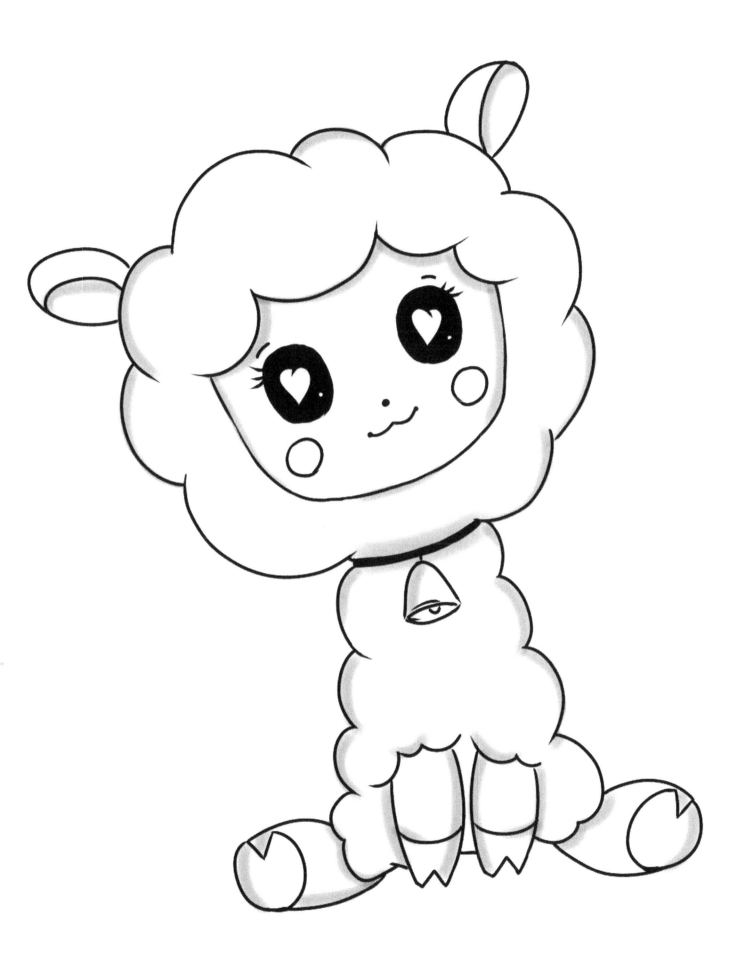

FREE PAGES FROM OUR BOOKS

THANK YOU for choosing our book, we hope you **LIKED IT**. Fill free to write **YOUR REVIEW** and show **YOUR ART-WORK** on **AMAZON**. We want to know **YOUR IMPRESSION** of the book.

And we want to **PRESENT YOU** pages from our other books:

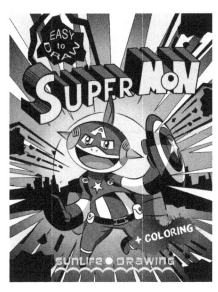
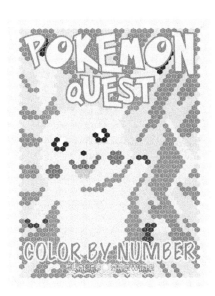
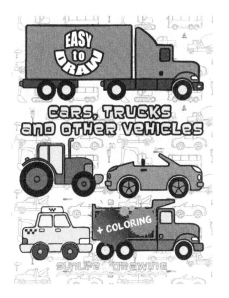

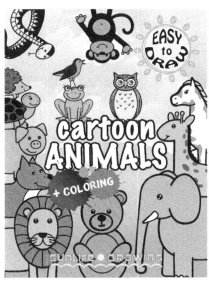
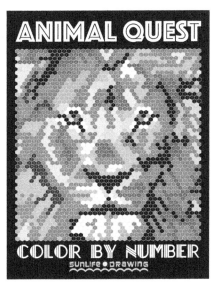
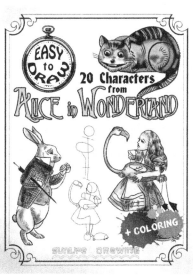

CaptainShtomp

1.

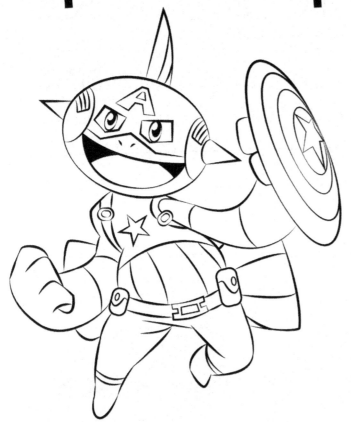 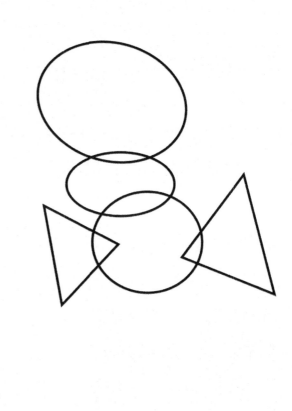

2.

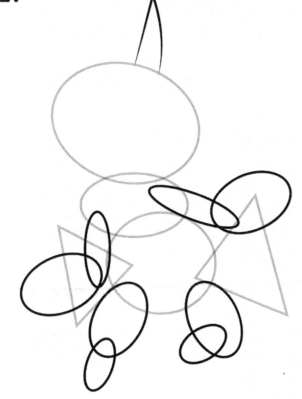

3.

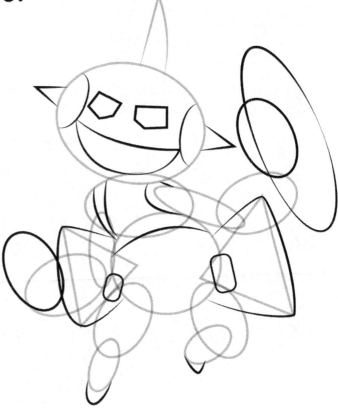

4.

5.

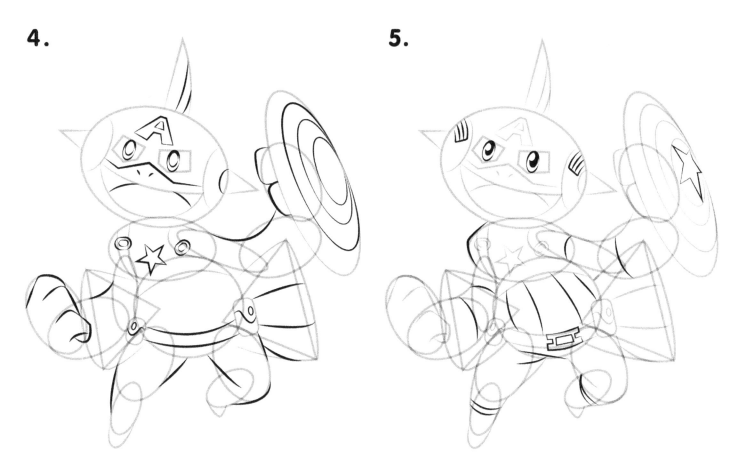

6.

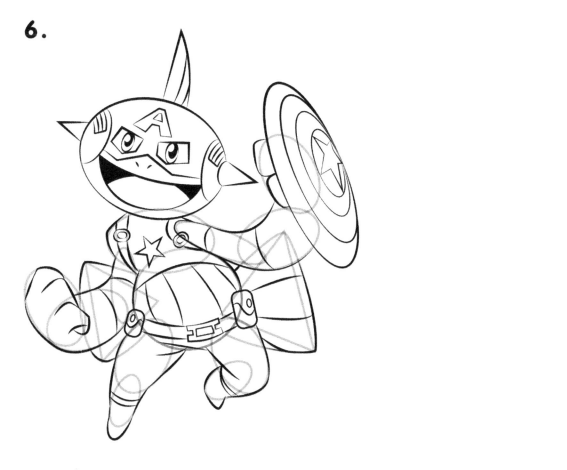

1	BLACK
2	GRAY
3	BROWN
4	RED
5	ORANGE
6	YELLOW
7	BRIGHT GREEN
8	GREEN
9	BLUE
10	SKY BLUE
11	PURPLE
12	PINK

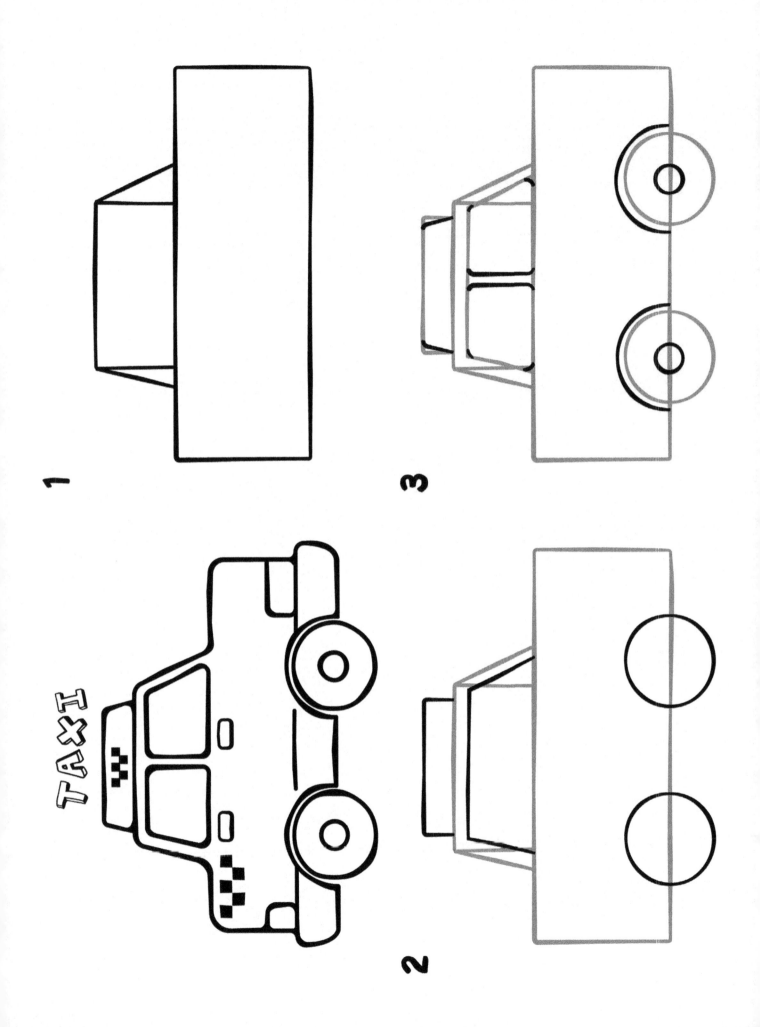

1

2

3

TAXI

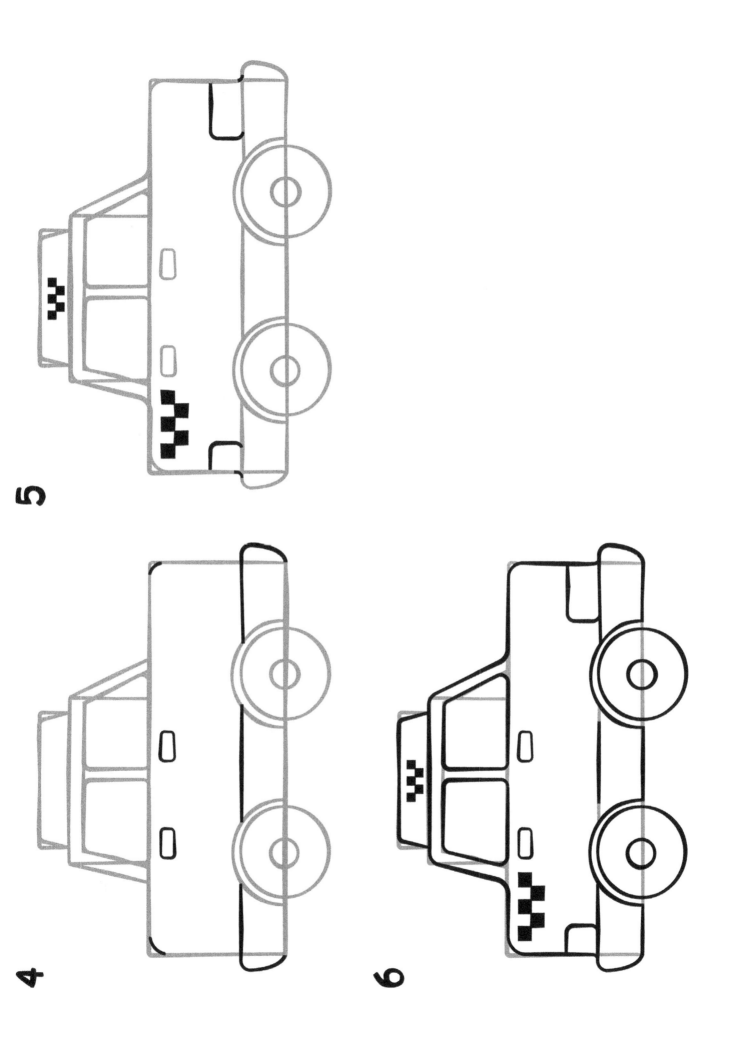

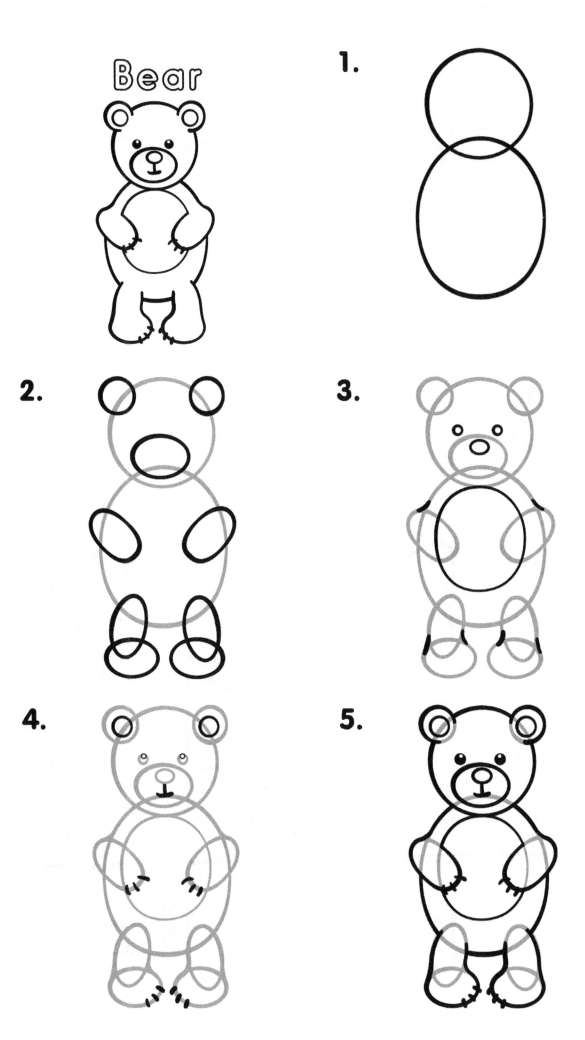

Bear

1.

2.

3.

4.

5.

Giraffe

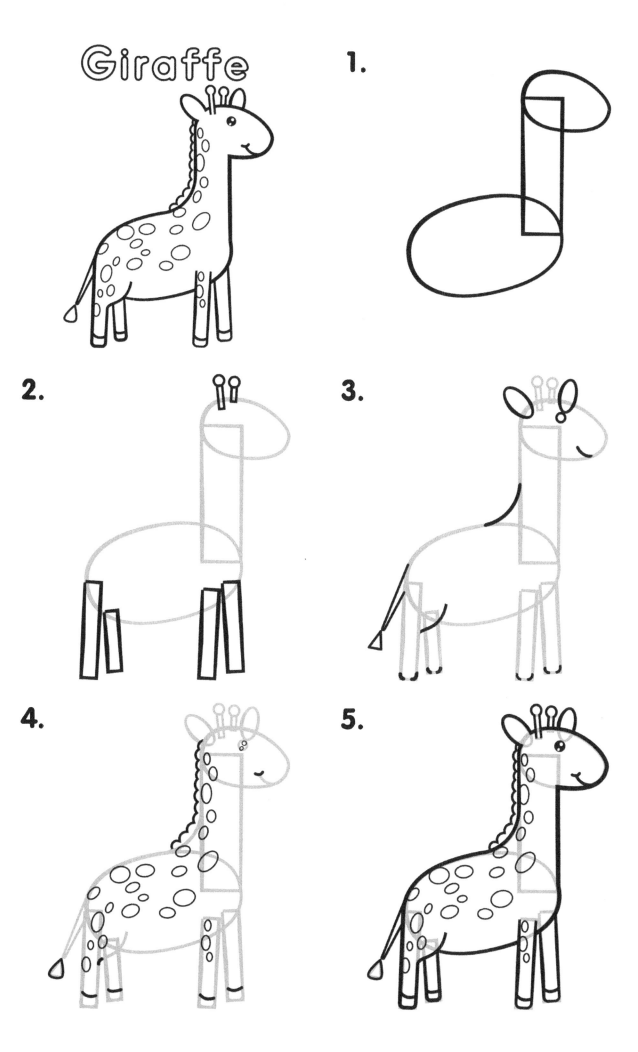

1.

2.

3.

4.

5.

1	BLACK
2	GRAY
3	BROWN
4	RED
5	ORANGE
6	YELLOW
7	BRIGHT GREEN
8	GREEN
9	BLUE
10	SKY BLUE
11	PURPLE
12	PINK

ALICE WITH FLAMINGO

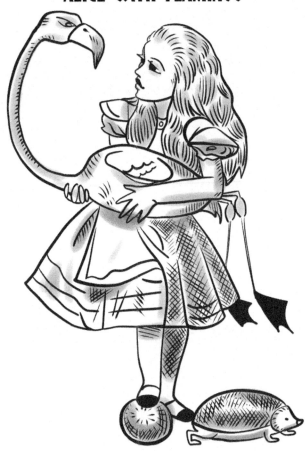

1.

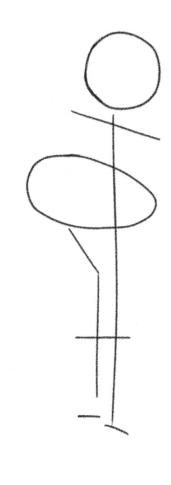

2.

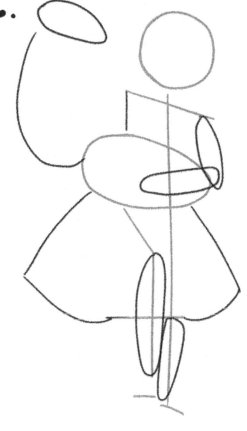

3.

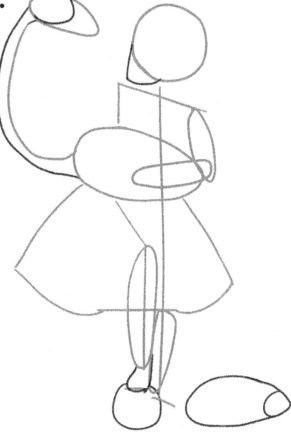

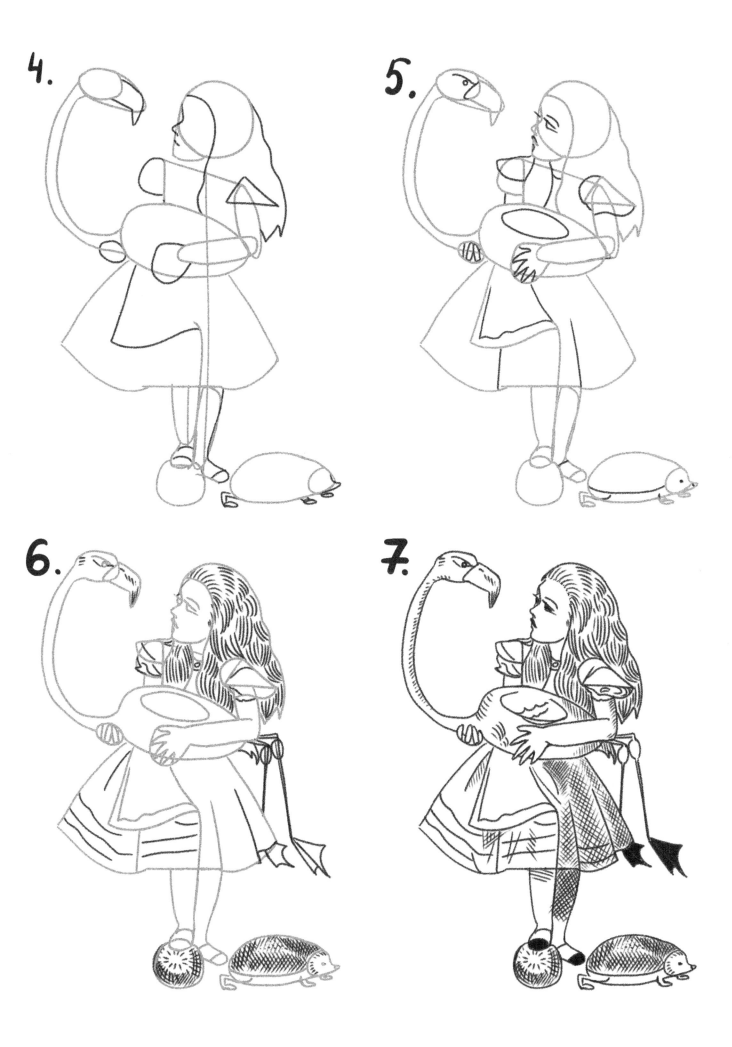

4.

5.

6.

7.

Made in the USA
Coppell, TX
27 March 2021